How Souls Grow

A Journalist
Interviews God on

How Souls Grow

in Faith, Hope,
and Love

Elaine McCreary

Copyright © 2025 by Elaine McCreary

All rights reserved. No part of this publication may be reproduced, stored in a retrieval system, or transmitted, in any form or by any means, except as may be expressly permitted by the 1976 Copyright Act or by the copyright holder in writing.

ISBN: 978-1-78324-379-2

Whilst every effort has been made to ensure that the information contained within this book is correct at the time of going to press, the author and publisher can take no responsibility for the errors or omissions contained within.

Book design by Wordzworth
www.wordzworth.com

CONTENTS

Preface: *Why send a journalist to interview God?*	ix
Introduction: *How will God reply to these questions?*	xi
1. WHO is this Soul Seeking Faith, Hope, and Love?	1
2. WHAT Process Develops the Soul?	13
3. WHY Is Such Transformation so All-Important?	31
4. WHEN Can Soul Progress Occur?	43
5. WHERE Will You Find Evidence of Spiritual Progress?	55
FAITH	71
6. HOW Does *Knowledge* Prepare Souls to Transform?	75
7. HOW Does *Volition* Free Souls to Transform?	89
8. HOW does ACTION Produce Transformation?	105
HOPE	115
9. HOW Does Divine Grace Make It All Possible?	119
LOVE	136
Epilogue	139
Glossary	141
Endnotes	147
Bibliography	155
About the Author	163

FAITH

Trust,

belief, reliance,

confidence, conviction,

spiritual apprehension.

HOPE

*Ambition,
aim, desire, plan,
aspiration, expectation,
to expect, anticipate, aspire.*

LOVE

Attraction, yearning, intimacy, attachment, compassion, care, kindness, benevolence.

PREFACE
Why send a journalist to interview God?

Before this project began, I was an academic, with lifetime tenure in an agricultural college, building new knowledge and skills in graduate students who were already professionals in international development, as it was practiced at that time. The field of practice was humanitarian and motivated by ideals, but for me something was missing. After seven years of research and teaching, sabbatical leave came due; and I took off to explore an absolutely burning question: How far can human learning reach?

I wanted to know why human beings are so curious, so hungry to know everything. "Everything" eventually takes us to the edge of the universe; and through its membrane out into the unmanifest cosmos, way out there – or way in here – depending on which way you are looking. Human beings want to know about our essence, and our purpose, and whether there is a way to transform from being limited and mortal, to being unlimited and endless.

Then one day, I came upon a radical quotation which led me to suspect that the purpose of existence, in all its complex beauty, has been to form an environment that would educate the souls of human beings. The quotation said:

> *"Out of the wastes of nothingness, with the clay of My command I made thee to appear and have ordained for thy training every atom in existence and the essence of all created things."*[1]

This Voice was asserting that human beings are supposed to learn from "every atom in existence" – which was handy—because this is what scientific search is all about! But it also referred to "training" and the "essence of all things"—which moves attention from sensory, material phenomena to the unmanifest noumena behind everything, from what is out there to what is in here - inside the learner—from external scientific search to internal spiritual search.

Then I came to a puzzle: **If** the training of every human soul is the underlying purpose of creation, **then** it would be *illogical* for the process to be so obscure that only a few, rarified human beings could undertake it. But, **if** the purpose is indeed to engage all human souls in spiritual training and transformation, **then** why have great literatures on spiritual development often been either so vague, or couched in such confounding language, that it seemed almost impossible for everyday human beings to grasp what this essential learning is all about, how it operates, and how we might cooperate with it?

The mysteries of spiritual learning and soul transformation continued to confound me as I pursued my chosen research; until one day, I was struck by virtual lightning after "ploughing through" over 90 volumes of Bahá'í Sacred Writings. (Please pardon the agricultural metaphor!) It suddenly occurred to me that the Divine would not quibble, or equivocate, if a humble journalist were to approach It with the six direct questions that are used to get every good story straight! So I decided to go into this research as a journalist daring to ask…

> If you don't mind, just the facts:
> WHO, WHAT, WHY, WHEN, WHERE and HOW
> can human souls grow in Faith, Hope, and Love?

INTRODUCTION
How will God reply to these questions?

If you are one of those rare individuals with advanced mystical capacities, you may feel that the answers you seek from It, arrive through your direct experience. If and when those answers come, they will be yours alone, non-transferable, non-replicable—since each mystic travels their own unique path.

For the rest of us, there are two "Books" publicly accessible. The first is the Book of nature, spread out all around and within us, having both visible and invisible patterns that reveal meanings to us. Scientists, artists, and lovers revel in nature, the great healer and model of harmony. Nature achieves harmony through predictable, reciprocal relations among forces and species. But humans are renegade.

A second Book is required for renegade humanity whose lack of understanding leads to misuse of that very same *free will* which is the distinguishing feature of their nobility. You observe nobility when a human being behaves harmoniously, not because they cannot do otherwise, but because they *choose* to do so; they *choose* to be good.

Throughout history, from age to age, Great Figures have appeared Who profoundly influenced human character and human society by revealing the direction of nobility. They achieved this influence through the revelation of Their lives and Their recorded teachings, contributing to the body of sacred writings that comprises a kind of planetary Book of wisdoms coming from the Source of all wisdom.

The purpose of this little volume is to attempt to demystify the arcane process of spiritual transformation by putting the journalist's questions to a new installment of the Book – a body of Sacred Writings emanating from three Central Figures of the Bahá'í Faith, the most recent, world-embracing spiritual community. These Central Figures are the Prophet-Herald (the Báb), the Prophet-Founder (Bahá'u'lláh), and 'Abdu'l-Bahá, who was appointed Centre of the Bahai community, and Interpreter of Bahá'í Sacred Writings, after the passing of Bahá'u'lláh. A few additional writings are included, where appropriate, from authorized institutions of the Faith, and occasionally from individual authors.

Rather than interrupt the flow of narration with explanations of historical figures or distinctly Bahá'í concepts, I have chosen to gather these descriptions into a Glossary at the back of the book, for the reader's convenient reference.

Personal Interpretation: Innumerable passages from Bahá'í Sacred Writings extol the "true seeker" who uses the powers of their rational soul to seek the Truth independently and find relevant meaning for themselves in Sacred Writings. As each person advances along their own unique path of spiritual discovery, they will interpret for themselves the clues and allusions they find in the Writings, and thus form their own impressions of the meaning to be found therein. This book records the contemplations and interpretations formed by the journalist while reviewing the quotations they gathered from Sacred Writings. The reader is, of course, invited to interpret all of those clues as seems sensible to them.

CHAPTER 1

WHO is this Soul Seeking Faith, Hope, and Love?

Beginning with Our Selves

So often we begin an exploration of the unknown by asking "what?" We ask, "What is it?" or "What happened?" or "What's going on?" as though by pointing out there, beyond ourselves, and asking "what?" we could find out everything we need to know. On that basis, it would be tempting to begin an enquiry into the subject of souls growing their capacities for faith, hope and love by asking the question "What is spiritual transformation?"

But transforming growth of a soul is a process, and such organic processes occur within living entities. To understand the processes of agriculture, we must first know the nature of plants; to understand the processes of human health promotion, we must first know the nature of human bodies; and to understand the processes of lifelong learning, we must first know something about the changing nature of human experience over a lifespan.

Therefore, when it comes to the process of soul development, we must first know something about the nature of a human soul, such as: What are its abilities? What is its potential for growth and influence? And what paradox may define the soul that lives in both visible and invisible worlds?

The Nature of Human Souls

Curiosity alone does not distinguish humans from animals since we see a marvelous curiosity in creatures from the octopus in the ocean to the chimpanzee on land, to the crow in the air. What we observe is that their explorations are externally directed to the things around them.

By contrast, human scientists, have been known to turn the spotlight of curiosity upon themselves, and ask "who are we that we want to probe all the secrets hidden in reality?" The very act of asking the question is the first clue to the answer. Humans are creatures who want to understand. The human culture of science itself is driven forward by irrepressible curiosity, the irresistible hunger to know—to know everything: to know what is true; to know what is right; to know what is hiding in everything we see around us.

Eventually the seeker will even seek its own origin, the source of itself, its point of creation. And if anyone should question personification of human origin as its "Creator," let them ask how their own personification could emerge from a Substance incapable of personification? Let them concede that the Substance from which human creativity emanates must be Itself Creative, whatever else It is. Consider:

> "First and foremost, among these favors, which the Almighty hath conferred upon man, is the gift of understanding. This gift giveth man the power to discern the truth in all things, leadeth him to that which is right, and helpeth him to discover the secrets of creation. His purpose in conferring such a gift is none other except to enable His creature to know and recognize the one true God — exalted be His glory."[2]

Here, Bahá'u'lláh confirms that the gift of understanding which drives the seeking soul to search for its impersonal Origin (or personalized Creator), was in fact implanted for just that purpose. The gift of understanding ensures that should we arrive at the journey's goal, we would be able to recognize completion and make the monumental transformation from being *seekers* to being *finders*, even when "finding" continues to deepen, expand and enrich without end.

It seems the Creator provided for endless enrichment of Its original creation, by adding the dimension of consciousness, awareness and understanding – thereby making Its creation into a "learning entity." For without this dimension, there would be nothing more to creation than a great whirling sculpture, a nursery-room mobile of cosmic proportions. But *with* this dimension comes the beginning of an entity no longer entirely unlike the Creator Itself, an entity embarked upon a process of selfhood, of deepening maturity, of endless elaboration.

The longest possible historical perspective, down the vistas of time, enables us to see the Inventor not just adding to the mass of cosmic existence, but constantly adding fresh vitality to it through this power of thought that It granted to souls and to the collective societies that these souls establish.

> "If we look objectively upon the world of being, it will become apparent that from age to age, the temple of existence has continually been embellished with a fresh grace, and distinguished with an ever-varying splendor, deriving from wisdom and the power of thought."[3]

But thought itself is preceded by a particular kind of perception that is more than just sensory perception – a perception which detects patterns, connections, relationships, and the rational order among them all.

> "All the sciences, branches of learning, arts, inventions, institutions, undertakings, and discoveries have resulted from the comprehension of the rational soul."[4]

However, "noblesse oblige" – meaning that the soul's nobility obligates it to exercise earnestly those very capacities to think, to investigate, and to understand. Although these capacities appear, at first, to be a simple gift, once having the ability of independent search, one has graduated forever beyond the instinctual, animal realm where mere imitation was sufficient to reach one's goal. The eagle, the wolf and the whale may imitate their ancestors; but the human soul must seek its goal, eagerly and anew with every generation, by a path no ancestor ever trod.

> "Furthermore, know ye that God has created in man the power of reason whereby man is enabled to investigate reality. God has not intended man to blindly imitate his fathers and ancestors... He must not be an imitator or blind follower of any soul. He must not rely implicitly upon the opinion of any man without investigation; nay, each soul must seek intelligently and independently, arriving at a real conclusion and bound only by that reality."[5]

This definitive capacity of thought, this signature endowment of the soul, does much more than merely complicate our existence while in mortal form. It is indeed the germ of our immortality.

Each living thing in creation brings forth fruit after its own kind, and the soul being essentially a locus of knowing, brings forth fruits of understanding. It possesses kaleidoscopic awareness eternally as its birthright from its God so that it constantly reviews and reconfigures its knowing to reveal new patterns and understandings.

> "All blessings are divine in origin, but none can be compared with this power of intellectual investigation and research which is an eternal gift producing fruits of

unending delight... All other blessings are temporary; this is an everlasting possession...it is an eternal blessing and divine bestowal, the supreme gift of God to man."[6]

Though endowed with this power tool of consciousness, each soul must independently learn to operate it, to exercise it, to direct it to undertake tasks, to choose a worthy mission. Many souls begin and end their incarnation on earth simply lost and disoriented—chasing after every possible commodity—without ever casting a thought to the question of their life, their purpose, their origin, their Source and Creator. Though the odds may be slim, some souls do undertake to track down the Creator. In His time, Lord Krishna was quoted as saying:

"Of many thousand mortals, one, perchance, striveth for Truth; and of those few that strive - nay, and rise high - one only...knoweth Me, as I am, the very Truth."[7]

That would make the odds of finding one's Origin, less than one-in-a-million. But it does assert that one soul consecrated to searching may rise high and progress in understanding. So it is that 'Abdu'l-Bahá states the value of a seeker when he says:

"One consecrated soul is preferable to a thousand other souls..."[8]

Sacred Writings recount that a consecrated soul, having found what it was seeking (its Source and true nature), dedicates itself to the Origin of its being. While lost, distracted and wandering souls dissipate their energies in chaotic directions, the soul who has found its Creator, aligns to that Source, and dedicates all its actions in that sacred direction, becoming attentive and responsive, so that the Creator in turn finds that soul desirable and prized.

The Nature of Souls when their Human Body Ceases to Exist

Here we begin by asking the basic question of whether the soul continues its life and learning after the physical body with which it has been associated ceases to exist. That inquiry yields a most interesting response:

> "And now concerning thy question regarding the soul of man and its survival after death. Know thou of a truth that the soul, after its separation from the body, will continue to progress until it attaineth the presence of God, in a state and condition which neither the revolution of ages and centuries, nor the changes and chances of this world, can alter."[9]

To appreciate how such an exalted continuity is possible, it will help us to consider the conditions that exist even when there is a living human body. Without careful investigation, one might imagine that a soul is contained in a human body in the same way that a mythical genie is contained within a bottle. But this is not so according to the authoritative Sacred Writings being investigated.

Instead, we find that while the powers of a soul, such as rationality or compassion, express themselves through the body with which it is associated, these powers are independent of the body. Using metaphors such as a lamp hidden under a bushel, or the sun hidden behind clouds, the principle is established that spiritual powers of the soul remain undiminished even if, for some reason, the body or mind are unable to express them.

> "Know thou that the soul of man is exalted above, and is independent of all infirmities of body or mind…the soul itself remaineth unaffected by any bodily ailments."[10]

Given this degree of independence, even while a physical body is in use, it seems that powers of a soul are even more unbounded when a physical human body no longer identifies a physical location for it.

"When it [the soul] leaveth the body, however, it will evince such ascendancy, and reveal such influence, as no force on earth can equal."[11]

Such a prospect is so inspiring, that one would want to make the best possible preparations while still living in this material world. Yet, there are so many options in this world, so many places to go, people to see, things to do, that a soul might find it overwhelming to choose a direction – except for one underlying dynamic. A soul searching for satisfaction will find all pathways frustrating except for finding one that leads homeward to its origin. Sacred Writings provide assurance that when a soul has found such a pathway, and followed it faithfully, it will find its journey is rewarded with success and satisfaction.

"Know thou, of a truth, that if the soul of man hath walked in the ways of God, it will, assuredly, return and be gathered to the glory of the Beloved…"[12]

Sacred Writings further indicate that a soul who has pursued its path of consecration in this life is destined to burst forth into spectacular, unimagined joyfulness beyond the limitations of earthly life.

Every pure, every refined and sanctified soul will be endowed with tremendous power and shall rejoice with exceeding gladness."[13]

Notice first that this passage indicates pre-conditions to be achieved, specifying that such souls as are "pure, refined, and sanctified" will rejoice with great gladness. Also eye-catching is the assertion that such a soul will acquire an astonishing capacity referred to as "tremendous power." This response to the interviewer's question about the potential of a soul after its physical body, is no doubt beyond the comprehension of we who are still living within the limitations of earthly life, but is still intriguing to us as an impenetrable enigma.

As we continue reading sacred descriptions of the soul's progress, we find it depicted as experiencing a kind of expansion or magnification in terms of both joy and power. One wonders what kind of power that might be. It seems that when a soul steadfastly follows its path of search to the end of its earthly life, the Creator may ennoble that soul in a manner that empowers it to be useful, to be a servant and benefactor to more worlds of God than this one.

> "The soul that hath remained faithful to the Cause of God, and stood unwaveringly firm in His Path shall, after his ascension, be possessed of such power that all the worlds which the Almighty hath created can benefit through him."[14]

The journalist notes that the foregoing passage does not say that all the worlds of God "will" benefit from that soul, rather there is something which makes such a soul potentially useful. Since we are unapprised of those other worlds, it is satisfying to ponder that such a soul can act as a servant of the Creator and do Its bidding in raising up and refining this present world from which it sprung.

> "Such a soul provideth, at the bidding of the Ideal King and Divine Educator, the pure leaven that leaveneth the world of being, and furnisheth the power through which the arts and wonders of the world are made manifest."[15]

It becomes apparent that Sacred Writings do not avoid our questions. Indeed, when we ask sincerely, without prejudice or presumption about what we may find, they provide answers that exceed our material capacity to comprehend, in the sense that they suggest possibilities far beyond the limitations of this mortal world. How can we in this world possibly imagine what the soul can become before we actually pass that way ourselves? While we live in this cloud-enshrouded world, seeing as *"through a glass darkly,"*[16] it's not surprising if we are unable to bear the thought of what such souls as described above can become.

A prime example of this challenge to our comprehension is the following statement from divine writings concerning the soul "when it leaveth the body." It begins with a common analogy about the light of the sun remaining undiminished even when obscured by an external impediment. Then it goes on to make an assertion about what the shining light of a free soul accomplishes.

> "Likewise, consider the sun which hath been obscured by the clouds. Observe how its splendor appeareth to have diminished, when in reality the source of that light hath remained unchanged. The soul of man should be likened unto this sun, and all things on earth should be regarded as his body. So long as no external impediment interveneth between them, the body will, in its entirety, continue to reflect the light of the soul, and to be sustained by its power."[17]

While the reader contemplates possible meanings of this passage, the journalist will press on to explore an interesting paradox concerning the soul.

The Paradox of the Soul

Here we come upon a seeming contradiction, a paradox of cosmic proportions. The foregoing Writings indicate that phenomenal expansion and unfoldment awaits the soul. Endless horizon upon horizon of becoming ever more enhanced. And yet, in the midst of this unbounded process, the soul is—purely, silently, forever—at rest. And this too is a gift of its Creator.

Bahá'u'lláh reveals that this paradox results from the soul concurrently living securely in the realm of eternity, while at the same moment, experiencing a world enchained to constantly changing contingencies. He states:

> "Verily I say, the human soul is exalted above all egress and regress. It is still, and yet it soareth; it moveth, and yet it is still. It is, in itself, a testimony that beareth witness to the existence of a world that is contingent, as well as to the reality of a world that hath neither beginning nor end."[18]

Without end, the essence of our own being remains beyond the grasp of our own minds, hearts, and souls. In subsequent chapters, we will consider evidence regarding behaviour of the soul in search for its own unfolding transformation. But the actual substance, the actual essence of the soul is as unknowable as the essence of God Itself—thereby leaving a clue that it has been produced from the same indivisible consciousness as its Origin.

> "Verily I say, the human soul is, in its essence, one of the signs of God, a mystery among His mysteries…Within it lieth concealed that which the world is now utterly incapable of apprehending."[19]

So, the interview begins by questioning the nature of souls and learning that Sacred Writings record how the soul is characterized by the capacity to think, explore, question, and continuously transcend its limitations. The soul can come to influence many other souls, the arts and sciences of human culture, and even the very matter which comprises this world and beyond. Yet, with all that potential to develop, the soul is forever mysteriously at rest.

Having established focus on this mysterious entity, the soul, the interviewer moves on to question the nature of spiritual transformation by which the soul will unfold its infinite potential.

CHAPTER 2

WHAT Process Develops the Soul?

In this scientific age, the rational soul in all of us requires a set of convictions about life that is based on evidence. We are not inclined to adopt a creed of faith based on some questionable claims, vague promises, or chilling threats. We are looking for spiritual practices that make sense to us, and lead us to experience a better life.

Our growing literacy about scientific cause-and-effect has led us to see everything as a process in which one phase or condition leads naturally to a subsequent one. Towards this end, the reader will find in this chapter a series of phases found in Bahá'í Sacred Writings concerning soul awareness. While making no claim to be exhaustive, the phases reported here are clear, inspiring and motivating. They include:

1. Personal purification
2. Awareness of a magnetic attraction to divine Love
3. Rotating to align to the attraction
4. Movement toward the attraction, and
5. Assimilation into the attraction

Our souls seem to experience each of these operations, or phases of that process, iteratively - that is, the stages keep occurring again and again – sometimes certain pairs of conditions repeating, sometimes the whole sequence repeating. It is not magic. It is not irrational. It is a logical series of conditions within the reach of every single human being – if and when they so choose.

Here are more detailed clues about each phase as they are found in Bahá'í Sacred Writings

Personal Purification

Purification, as the essential prerequisite for spiritual awakening to begin, is described with variations in *every* religious practice on earth. Of itself, earthly life drags us into thoughtless habits of behaviour that keep our soul bound to, and limited by, the physical, material, and mortal side of our nature. Therefore, to awaken and activate the conscious, transcendent, and immortal side of our nature, a human being must begin by eliminating numerous worldly fixations and identifications.

To purify one's behaviour toward others, it would clearly help to monitor and purify one's pattern of speech. And to purify speech sincerely, would require one to purify their thoughts. But to purify thoughts, one would have to deal with their all-powerful precursor – and that is "perception."

What we perceive by seeing, hearing, or feeling, becomes the substance upon which our thoughts operate. So, it comes as a radical discovery when we realize that what we *think* we perceive "out there" is not so much a function of something that actually is out there, as it is a function of what we are prepared "in here" to recognize, to acknowledge, to admit.

By stages, it is possible to eliminate many internal layers of preconceptions and misconceptions about daily life. Initially we may have thought that life conditions are due to the actions of other people, or of social trends, or our own prior behaviour; and consequently, that conditions are somewhat random. But at later stages of purification, we may come to perceive that conditions are not so much random, as they are purposeful, and result in education of the soul. If conditions are *conducive* to human nobility, then we learn to continue there. If conditions are *counter* to human nobility, then we learn we must change something both courageously and forcefully.

So it was that the Báb, when preparing the way for humanity to receive a new vision of themselves, emphasized the initial action of purification, as set out in His work, the Bayan:

> "Know thou that in the Bayán *purification* is
> regarded as the most acceptable means for attaining
> nearness unto God and as the most meritorious
> of all deeds. Thus, purge thou thine ear
> that thou mayest hear no mention besides God,
> and purge thine eye that it behold naught except God,
> and thy conscience that it perceive
> naught other than God,
> and thy tongue that it proclaim nothing but God,
> and thy hand to write naught but the words of God,
> and thy knowledge that it comprehend
> naught except God,
> and thy heart that it entertain no wish save God."[20]

Gradually, as the soul continues this process of purifying its perception, by seeing within external conditions their divine purpose, then the soul begins to feel differently about its human life. It finds itself living in a benevolent environment that is suited to educate, and ultimately liberate, the soul.

In the 19th century, when the Báb delivered the foregoing directive on purification, the world was feverishly expecting the arrival of a great, divine Educator. The Báb was advising attracted souls that purification of perception would not only improve their daily life immediately, but also prepare and qualify them, when the time came, to recognize that greater Educator to whom He referred as "Him Whom God shall make manifest."

> "...and in like manner purge all thine acts and thy pursuits that thou mayest be nurtured in the paradise of pure love, and perchance mayest attain the presence of Him Whom God shall make manifest, adorned with a purity which He highly cherisheth, and be sanctified from whosoever hath turned away from Him and doth not support Him. Thus, shalt thou manifest a purity that shall profit thee."[21]

When the greater Manifestation did appear, in the divine figure of Bahá'u'lláh, He repeated the theme of purifying perceptions and emphasized the sweet benefits that would flow from such perceptions and
bring seekers to a new knowledge.

> "O Lord of all being and Educator of all things visible and invisible! Grant us ears that are pure, hearts that are sanctified, and eyes that see, so that we may discover the sweetness of Thine enthralling utterance, may fix our gaze upon Thy supreme horizon, and may come to know whatever hath been sent down through Thy bounty..."[22]

Although less often mentioned than the analogies of sight or hearing, Sacred Writings even refer to the sense of smell as a spiritual means for a seeking soul to perceive the divine. Pursuing those sensations of divine perfume ultimately will lead the soul to its heavenly destination.

> "When the channel of the human soul is cleansed of all worldly and impeding attachments, it will unfailingly perceive the breath of the Beloved across immeasurable distances, and will, led by its perfume, attain and enter the City

of Certitude...Its wondrous tulips unfold the mystery of the undying Fire in the Burning Bush, and its sweet savors of holiness breathe the perfume of the Messianic Spirit."[23]

Today, as in the past, the process of purifying perception enables the soul to find unity and harmony in its surroundings, and concurrently to achieve an internal, personal integrity. Thoughts, speech, character, and behaviour begin to reinforce each other in a daily life purified of the extraneous, and coherent in its sense of dignity and purpose.

"...man's supreme honour and real happiness lie in self-respect, in high resolves and noble purposes, in integrity and moral quality, in immaculacy of mind."[24]

That the process of purification is satisfying and gratifying in itself is more than enough compensation for the fact that it is never complete. In this world, the downward pull of material thinking is always present, providing a constant stimulus to be vigilant in one's practice of purification.

"...the complete and entire elimination of the ego would imply perfection – which man can never completely attain – but the ego can and should be ever-increasingly subordinated to the enlightened soul of man. This is what spiritual progress implies."[25]

As perceptions are purified, a second phase becomes possible.

Awareness of the Magnetic Attraction of Divine Love

Over time, more refined perceptions may lead a soul to make daily choices that support the quality of life it is beginning to enjoy.

Gradually an underlying feeling may take hold. A soul may become aware of some sensation that resembles benevolence, good will, loving care and empathy. A soul may begin to notice something that permeates all its random thoughts and has an appeal that draws its attention. What is it? Where is it coming from? Perhaps this stimulus takes decades to arise; perhaps it takes a hundred thousand random thoughts; but somewhere along the way, any given soul may begin to realize that this is the sensation of divine Love – a warm, lively, engaging embrace that protects one from all fear, and draws one into fulfilment of all desire.

While soul awareness varies with each individual, the sensations described above first happened to this author as a young mother, holding my newborn first baby, as I stood in the archway leading to our kitchen. I was gazing with complete amazement into her perfect little face trying to fathom how each detail could be so artistically refined, when a drop of milk emerged from a corner of that little rosebud mouth. At that moment, when the old me might have said "this is imperfect; this is an error that needs to be blotted with a cloth" – instead – a thundering force like Niagara Falls came powering through me toward that baby and crowned that drop of milk with perfection, and that mouth, and that cheek, and those eyes, and that forehead. I was stunned. I could only think "This must be the Love of God Itself for this newborn, for I have never in my life felt anything remotely like this."

Such divine Love permeates and saturates and elevates all "phenomena" into their original "noumena" and reveals the transcendent that lives just behind the immanent. Such divine Love is the ultimate solvent, the elixir that dissolves all fragmented things into one Reality. Such Love is the one revelation that makes everything else clear and meaningful.

> "Know thou of a certainty that Love is the secret of God's holy Dispensation, the manifestation of the All-Merciful, the fountain of spiritual outpourings."[26]

Such Love illuminates everything, energizes life and brings clarity to consciousness. It is a unifier that leaves no thing, no condition, no experience, no lesson, no regret – nothing – remaining outside the realm of spiritually meaningful life.

> "Love is heaven's kindly light, the Holy Spirit's eternal breath that vivifieth the human soul. Love is the cause of God's revelation unto man, the vital bond inherent, in accordance with the divine creation, in the realities of things."[27]

That such Love is a bonding or binding force is evidenced at the largest cosmic levels as well as the smallest sub-atomic levels, and everything in between such as the experience of human beings as they cultivate their soul progress. It seems futile at this time of writing to debate whether that bonding and binding force is magnetic or gravitational, since human science is still struggling today to conceptualize a unified field theory. Instead, let us just contemplate the formidable, macroscopic effect of the force of Love as described in the following passage:

> "Love is the most great law that ruleth this mighty and heavenly cycle, the unique power that bindeth together the divers elements of this material world, the supreme magnetic force that directeth the movements of the spheres in the celestial realms."[28]

Having once felt that undeniable, spiritual force of attraction, the soul begins eagerly searching around for the origin, in to order to experience more of that sensation!

Rotating to Align to the Attraction

At first, the soul may think that these occasional sensations of divine, disinterested, and unconditional Love are just an unpredictable phenomenon beyond the range of its individual control.

But a little experimentation, through prayer or meditation, will reveal that it **is** possible to increase both the frequency and the intensity of these experiences by "turning toward" or "attuning to" the sensation when it occurs.

Bahá'í Sacred Writings contain explicit directions on how to follow that signal, and turn toward its divine Source – such as the following examples:

> "Place, in all circumstances, thy whole trust in Thy Lord, and fix thy gaze upon Him, and turn away from all them that repudiate His truth."[29]

> "Turn thy face unto Mine and renounce all save Me; for My sovereignty endureth and My dominion perisheth not. If thou seekest another than Me, yea, if thou searchest the universe forevermore, thy quest will be in vain."[30]

> "Turn thy face to the divine Kingdom and strive that thou mayest acquire merciful characteristics, mayest become illumined and acquire the attributes of the Kingdom and of the Lord."[31]

After realizing that attunement to this signal is important for expanding spiritual awareness, the soul becomes inspired to ask for help to accomplish alignment. The seeker who has yet to find their powerful "North star" or their "magnetic North pole," may still have realized that every capacity to think, to learn, to seek, to advance, indeed all capacities are not inherent within their human frame but within the consciousness of the One Who is their Source. Therefore, the seeker communicates to the Source that it wants more of that signal of divine love using phrases such as the following:

WHAT PROCESS DEVELOPS THE SOUL?

"...aid me to turn my face towards Thy face, to fix mine eyes upon Thee, and to speak of Thy glory."[32]

"Unlock before my face the doors of abundance, grant me deliverance, and sustain me, through means I cannot reckon, from the treasuries of heaven. Suffer me to turn my face toward the countenance of Thy generosity and to be entirely devoted to Thee, O Thou Who art merciful and compassionate!"[33]

"Thou art He, O my Lord, Who hath called Himself the God of Mercy, the Most Compassionate. Have mercy, then, upon Thy handmaiden who hath sought Thy shelter, and set her face towards Thee."[34]

"Unto Thee be praise for that Thou hast enraptured me by the sweetness of Thine utterances and set me towards the horizon above which the splendors of the Daystar of Thy face have shone and caused me to turn unto Thee at a time when most of Thy creatures had broken off from Thee."[35]

Having begun to turn into alignment with that signal of divine Love, the seeker begins to realize that turning towards something means concurrently that it will be voluntarily turning away from something else. It is a choice. Every choice for one thing is an un-choice of the alternative.

This is the real beginning of self-chosen spiritual advancement.

"O friend, till thou enter the garden of these inner meanings, thou shalt never taste of the imperishable wine of this valley. And shouldst thou taste of it, thou wilt turn away from all else and drink of the cup of contentment; thou wilt loose thyself from all things and bind thyself unto Him..."[36]

> "...it behooves man to abandon thoughts of nonexistence and death, which are absolutely imaginary, and see himself ever-living, everlasting in the divine purpose of his creation. He must turn away from ideas which degrade the human soul so that day by day and hour by hour he may advance upward and higher to spiritual perception of the continuity of the human reality."[37]

Indeed, this self-chosen act of turning away from previously desired things, and turning toward the enchanting sensation of divine love, is the operational definition of "repenting" or "repentance." The "turning" does not mean, as commonly assumed, that repentance is merely remorse or regret for degrading acts one may have committed. The term includes both the notion of changing one's mind as well as changing one's behaviour and direction. Whether one feels remorse for having been culpable in an injustice, or regret for having wasted one's life and capacity, turning *away* is only the beginning of the turn. Turning *toward*, brings an additional meaning.

The completion of the turn occurs when one's sensations are filled with the greater Reality that successfully displace the former habits of thought and behaviour. This exchange is called "redemption." One redeems (meaning "exchanges") a lesser thing, a token or a voucher, for a real thing such as a free coffee, or a door prize at an event. The greatest redemption of all is to exchange belief in mortal human life for an awareness of spiritual life that will be never-ending and filled with the bestowals of a generous divine Host.

> "...haply ye may ask forgiveness of Him, may return unto Him, may truly repent, may realize your misdeeds, may shake off your slumber, may be roused from your heedlessness, may atone for the things that have escaped you, and be of them that do good...and return ye to God

and repent, that He, through His grace, may have mercy upon you, may wash away your sins, and forgive your trespasses."[38]

"Beseech thou the One true God that He may enable everyone to repent and return unto Him."[39]

"Cast away, therefore, the mere conceit thou dost follow, for mere conceit can never take the place of truth. Be thou of them that have truly repented and returned to God, the God Who hath created thee, Who hath nourished thee, and made thee a minister among them that profess thy faith."[40]

Being immersed in that sensation of an anonymous, all-pervading Love becomes a kind of homing-beam for the rest of one's life. To re-align in this way is the true mean of "religion"—to re-align oneself toward the divine. Its taste is more desirable, more appealing than any other gratification, and following it naturally becomes a commitment, a first nature. But having re-aligned oneself is not the end. What ensues is a forward movement in that direction.

Movement toward the Attraction

The process of "redemption" that has been initiated (exchanging former states of being for new states) creates a sensation of motion, whereby one leaves behind undesirable experiences and focuses instead on more attractive experiences. This can also be understood as an operation of detachment from old habits and attachment to new aspects of life. As the soul learns, it moves. This is the motion of its life.

"Now let us consider the soul. We have seen that movement is essential to existence; nothing that has life is without motion. All creation, whether of the mineral, vegetable or animal kingdom, is compelled to obey the law of motion; it must either ascend or descend. But with the human soul, there is no decline. Its only movement is towards perfection; growth and progress alone constitute the motion of the soul."[41]

This does not guarantee that behaviour will always improve. At times, human behaviour can deteriorate; but the soul itself never forgets the level of divine life it has tasted. It will never again be satisfied with anything less. The soul's movement toward perfection is therefore not as smooth as the growth of a plant; rather it may at times resemble the tired plodding of a pilgrim. We find this human perseverance described by such figures of speech as "treading a path" or "scaling heights."

> "Were he that treadeth the path of guidance and seeketh to scale the heights of righteousness to attain unto this glorious and exalted station, he would inhale, at a distance of a thousand leagues, the fragrance of God, and would perceive the resplendent morn of a Divine guidance rising above the dayspring of all things."[42]

Holding tightly to that sensation of divine Love is like holding onto an invisible cord that guides one in the forward motion of self-development and soul progress.

> "Love is the light that guideth in darkness, the living link that uniteth God with man, that assureth the progress of every illumined soul."[43]

When the soul's progress is augmented by divine grace, it can occur with rapidity, making up for what now seem like years of life lost in a world of experiences which were remote from this desired goal. Now, the soul wants to be closer to the heart of things, to be at the very centre of Reality, as quickly as possible. And there is assurance that such rapid advancement is possible.

> "Be self-sacrificing in the path of God and wing thy flight unto the heavens of the love of the Abha Beauty, for any movement animated by love moveth from the periphery to the centre, from space to the Day-Star of the universe. Perchance thou deemest this to be difficult, but I tell thee that such cannot be the case, for when the motivating and guiding power is the divine force of magnetism it is possible, by its aid, to traverse time and space easily and swiftly."[44]

The closer it attains to its goal, the more is the soul filled with the presence of the Divine and finds itself joyfully plunging into the sensation of divine love.

Assimilation into the Attraction of Love

As the "movement" of spiritual progress begins to draw each soul closer toward the Centre of divine love, the individual discovers that its sense of identity is changing. Awareness of a soul-Self is now filling the space of consciousness that used to be occupied by an ego-centred self. The new soul-Self is communing in its empathic heart with the very Spirit of Love.

Our first thoughts about "purification" may focus on externalities such as clutter, dirt, and unworthy speech and behaviour. As these externalities are "purified" by such verbs as cleanse, purge, or wash away, we may then begin to contemplate the essential substance itself, which is the human heart in its original state before those externalities were layered onto it. Here we may come to realize that it was always untainted, refined or sanctified (the latter term meaning to be sacred as its Origin is sacred)—a single, conscious substance, indivisible, and therefore eternal.

In many religious traditions, it is asserted that the Creator has a claim upon the heart, the location of empathic communication. It is the one place in creation where the Divine will talk with the seeker.

> "All that is in heaven and earth I have ordained for thee, except the human heart, which I have made the habitation of My beauty and glory..."[45]

Sacred Writings seem to indicate that as the soul dwells upon sensations that it is experiencing in the inner sanctum of the human heart, it may come to feel its own qualities becoming more refined, purified and sanctified, better able to reflect its Creator. The soul feels with a greater intensity, as though it were actually moving toward, or deeper into, divine presence.

Here we come upon a subtle redefinition of "movement." A soul's movement does not proceed like a person crossing a room toward a grand piano where an accomplished musician is playing. In crossing the room, that person would not themselves become a musician. In other words, they do not transform. By contrast, spiritual transformation proceeds more like a diver returning from deep in the ocean (of material consciousness) and rising toward the sunshine-sparkled waters (of spiritual consciousness) higher, near the ocean's surface. The diver must rise *gradually* through the many layers of specific density of ocean waters. As divers rise, their own specific density changes; they themselves become lighter and so can bear the experience of higher waters. So it is that movement of the soul is defined by progressive purification and unfoldment of spiritual qualities. This may unfold what is meant by "nearness is likeness."

> "Therefore, we learn that nearness to God is possible through devotion to Him, through entrance into the Kingdom and service to humanity; it is attained by unity

with mankind and through loving-kindness to all; it is dependent upon investigation of truth, acquisition of praiseworthy virtues, service in the cause of universal peace, and personal sanctification. In a word, nearness to God necessitates sacrifice of self, severance and the giving up of all to Him. Nearness is likeness."[46]

In the fundamental assertion that spiritual transformation is a process accessible to every willing human being, the following excerpt helps us to define simply and yet precisely, what the "image and likeness of God" implies. As God Itself is unknowable, our only approach is through the divine qualities, virtues or perfections we associate with Its saints and holy ones.

"Let us now discover more specifically how he is the image and likeness of God and what is the standard or criterion by which he can be measured and estimated. This standard can be no other than the divine virtues which are revealed in him. Therefore, every man imbued with divine qualities, who reflects heavenly moralities and perfections, who is the expression of ideal and praiseworthy attributes, is, verily, in the image and likeness of God. If a man possesses wealth, can we call him an image and likeness of God? Or is human honor and notoriety the criterion of divine nearness?"[47]

In parallel fashion, the rational soul explores material reality by developing scientific disciplines, and explores divine virtues by developing disciplines of self-mastery. In this way, the soul becomes immersed in, and filled with, the Love that is God and progressively foregoes the material nature that humans share with animals.

"As he possesses sense endowment in common with the animals, it is evident that he is distinguished above them by his conscious power of penetrating abstract realities. He acquires divine wisdom; he searches out the mysteries of creation; he witnesses the radiance of omnipotence; he attains the second birth—that is to say, he is born out of the material world just as he is born of the mother; he attains to everlasting life; he draws nearer to God; his heart is replete with the love of God. This is the foundation of the world of humanity; this is the image and likeness of God; this is the reality of man; otherwise, he is an animal."[48]

It is explicitly stated that this spiritual self-mastery is the intended pursuit of all souls, whether their human lives are lived as men or women.

"Know thou, O handmaid, that in the sight of Bahá, women are accounted the same as men, and God hath created all humankind in His own image, and after His own likeness. That is, men and women alike are the revealers of His names and attributes, and from the spiritual viewpoint there is no difference between them. Whosoever draweth nearer to God, that one is the most favored, whether man or woman."[49]

Across the planet, the human race has a unique relationship with all other forms of life. The human being resembles the animal kingdom in many respects but is also endowed with features and capacities beyond its mortal, animal life which keep the soul in a constant state of creative tension. For this reason, the Divine Educators come to assist, guide, and accompany the impatient soul as it finds its way.

"Man is in the ultimate degree of materiality and the beginning of spirituality; that is, he is at the end of imperfection and the beginning of perfection… He has both an animal side and an angelic side, and the role of the educator is to so train human souls that the angelic side may overcome the animal."[50]

As with all living beings that grow, expand, and mature in a gradual process, human souls also require time for the gradual emergence of their full awareness and unfoldment of their capacities. Emerging souls can benefit from the assistance of beings with higher consciousness who understand what is required to ensure fulfilment of the spiritual process. So it is that souls seek guidance from the most inspiring beings they can find, the greatest of whom are the exceedingly rare, Manifestations who are especially suited to be the divine Gardeners of human soul consciousness.

"That is to say, the teachings of Christ and the Prophets are necessary for his [the soul's] education and guidance. Why? Because They are the divine Gardeners Who till the earth of human hearts and minds. They educate man, uproot the weeds, burn the thorns and remodel the waste places into gardens and orchards where fruitful trees grow. The wisdom and purpose of Their training is that man must pass from degree to degree of progressive unfoldment until perfection is attained."[51]

How arduous and lengthy this process of soul transformation seems to be! How great the perseverance that is required even to contemplate, let alone undertake, this spiritual path. Such an undertaking will require compelling motivations that can sweep away all hesitation and answer the priority question: WHY is such transformation so all-important?"

CHAPTER 3

WHY Is Such Transformation so All-Important?

At first glance, it would seem self-evident that to transform from identifying as a body that dies, to identifying as a soul that has endless possibilities, would be a good thing. But that process of spiritual transformation also seems to be difficult, challenging, even all-consuming. Therefore, in order to unleash sufficient motivating drive to launch into this process, souls require clarity about the purpose and impacts that make it so all-important. This chapter highlights a surprising range of outcomes: to develop noble qualities within the soul, to fulfil the mission of the soul and the purpose of creation, to attain a new form of salvation and spiritualize human civilization, and even to "solace the eyes" of the Creator Itself - a formidable range of heroic outcomes - that will indeed intensify motivation. Let us begin with the most apparent effect, which is to develop noble qualities.

To Develop Noble Qualities

Humans growing from childhood to youth, to young adulthood, experience a notable expansion of capacities. The simplest form is automatic growth in stature, strength, and sexual maturity. More demanding is a range of cultural capacities from sports to music to academics that require willpower, practice, and determination. Beyond those two forms of growth in capacity is yet another form that is sometimes described as spiritual progress.

> "Progress is of two kinds: material and spiritual. The former is attained through observation of the surrounding existence and constitutes the foundation of civilization. Spiritual progress is through the breaths of the Holy Spirit and is the awakening of the conscious soul of man to perceive the reality of Divinity. Material progress ensures the happiness of the human world. Spiritual progress ensures the happiness and eternal continuance of the soul."[52]

This awakening can also be termed spiritual development – not the false "development" such as occurs when one culture forces a foreign political economy onto another – but a true development which occurs from within. The term development derives from the French term "voleper" which expresses the concept of wrapping as with a rose bud. To "de-voleper" then means to unwrap something inherent that was always there but not yet made apparent. Spiritual development thus would indicate the unwrapping of spiritual potential, the unfolding of the blossom of soul qualities.

Among the noble qualities that the soul begins to unfold from within itself are those that go far beyond its own happiness and tranquility. Altruistic qualities begin to spread abroad in service to other people within their sphere. By touching more hearts and providing benefit to them, the soul experiences greater degrees of fulfilment.

> And the honor and distinction of the individual consist in this, that he among all the world's multitudes should become a source of social good. Is any larger bounty conceivable than this, that an individual, looking within

himself, should find that by the confirming grace of God he has become the cause of peace and well-being, of happiness and advantage to his fellow men? No, by the one true God, there is no greater bliss, no more complete delight."[53]

Beyond simply unwrapping quality after quality, or adding capacity to capacity, you might wonder if there are more comprehensive reasons why soul progress is so important. And there are.

To Fulfil the Mission of a Soul and the Purpose of Creation

When we look upon all existence, we see in each existing thing a distinctive, identifying characteristic. For example, rivers display humility by seeking the lowest point; mountains display steadfastness by enduring against eroding forces; trees display patience by growing slowly. As each and every existing quality emerged from the same Origin, it is referred to, in spiritual discourse, as being one of the innumerable "names" or attributes of God. The exposition is put forth that human consciousness is unique in that it encompasses not only the qualities of mineral, vegetable, and animal domains, but that in reaching across the cosmos (and indeed into the invisible beyond the visible aspects of reality), soul consciousness can reflect *all* the names of God.

> "Now, the world of existence, indeed every created thing, proclaims but one of the names of God, but the reality of man is an all-encompassing and universal reality which is the seat of the revelation of all the divine perfections. That is, a sign of each one of the names, attributes, and perfections that we ascribe to God exists in man. If such were not the case, he would be unable to imagine and comprehend these perfections."[54]

Here it can be seen that each soul is not required to become a scientist, philosopher or famous mystic, but simply to live a life of wonder, marveling at all the attributes of creation that it does appreciate; and realizing that behind each and every marvel lies an awesome Oneness. Happy the soul that realizes all creation lives within its awareness.

The exposition goes even further to posit that if humanity were not existing for the purpose of seeing all the manifested names of God, to "reflect" them in wonderment back at the Creator, then creation itself would be pointless. So critical is this capacity of humankind to reflect the totality of creation that one could say that creation did not really exist until it could be seen by human consciousness. — For those who say human beings appeared on earth long after creation and evolution of the planet, the response is "yes, of course." But the cosmos itself was in existence long before earth began to emerge and human consciousness is now following cosmic lights back to their source, becoming ever more present to observe earliest emergence of the cosmos.

> "Thus man is a perfect mirror facing the Sun of Truth and is the seat of its reflection… If man did not exist, the universe would be without result, for the purpose of existence is the revelation of the divine perfections. We cannot say, then, that there was a time when man was not. At most we can say that there was a time when this earth did not exist, and that at the beginning man was not present upon it."[55]

The capacity to reflect in amazement upon all the wonders in the world and beyond, the desire to trace these wonders back through cause-and-effect to their Source, these capacities and desires may be termed "science" but they could just as easily be termed "love." Indeed some texts refer to this love and wonderment as "worship" which is a mingling of conscious amazement and praise. Some call this mutual communication of generating creation followed by responding in worship, as "communion."

Such interwoven communion between Creator and soul awareness may rightly be understood as the very purpose of initiating creation.

"Having created the world and all that liveth and moveth therein, He, through the direct operation of His unconstrained and sovereign Will, chose to confer upon man the unique distinction and capacity to know Him and to love Him—a capacity that must needs be regarded as the generating impulse and the primary purpose underlying the whole of creation…" [56]

While marveling at features of the cosmos and its overwhelming unity, human souls may shy away from direct communion with its unifying perfection because they are painfully aware of what feels like their own imperfections, their pettiness, their failings, and their faults. This sense of human unworthiness imposes a false distance and fear of communion even when one senses a divine invitation, as expressed by Adam when he is quoted as saying:"*…I heard thy voice in the garden, and I was afraid, because I was naked; and I hid myself.*"[57] No human soul feels it can close the distance between its partialness and the unifying Oneness behind all things. Only Oneness Itself could dispel the human sense of not belonging, of having broken off, of being vulnerable and afraid, and of needing to be saved.

To Attain a New Salvation

Well before its use by Christian thinkers, the term salvation conveyed concepts of health and safety, some of which continue to this day as illustrated by a secular statement such as: *Forgiveness of her student loan was her financial salvation.* This is not a misuse, but rather an original use of the term. Origins of the term salvation can be traced back through Middle English to Latin *salvus*[58] meaning safe/healthy.

Woven into the urgent need for salvation were many forms of threat. Salvation was cast as preservation from destruction or failure, and deliverance from danger or difficulty, harm, ruin, or loss. One could say, for example: *Salvation of the trade route was achieved by the presence of many lighthouses to protect merchant ships from being shattered on rocky shores.*

The notion of salvation as protection or preservation of the soul is found in Bahá'í Sacred Writings as the means of deliverance for each soul from its own ignorance or illusion, fear or sorrow, back into communion with its Source. Though not heard frequently in Bahá'í conversations, the term can be found early in the Bahá'í era in this prayer of the Báb.

> "O Lord! Thou art the Remover of every anguish and the Dispeller of every affliction. Thou art He Who banisheth every sorrow and setteth free every slave, the Redeemer of every soul. O Lord! Grant deliverance through Thy mercy, and reckon me among such servants of Thine as have gained salvation."[59]

In some circles, Christian theologians applied the term salvation to mean deliverance from sin (an offence) and its consequences (punishment). They also tended to attribute that deliverance to the blood sacrifice of Jesus—a traditional practice of ending the life of an innocent substitute such as a dove or a lamb, so that the troubled supplicant could attain freedom from the consequences of bad actions, and attain a better life for themselves. The tradition evolved to assert that an individual could attain safety (salvation) not by changing themselves and sacrificing their own former choices to better ones, but rather by laying claim to the sacrifice already made by Jesus through association with, or faith in, Him. This could be demonstrated by physically imbibing a dark liquid symbolic of blood.

WHY IS SUCH TRANSFORMATION SO ALL-IMPORTANT?

Poetically, Bahá'í Sacred Writings also speak of drinking.

> "Seize ye the chalice of salvation at this dawntide in the name of Him Who causeth the day to break and drink your fill in praise of Him Who is the All-Glorious, the Incomparable."[60]

But what is it that souls are being called to drink? And how? In a higher level of transcendent abstraction, it is the rational soul that is drinking, the individual mind or spiritual consciousness. What is being imbibed into awareness is spiritual wisdom found in the chalice of revealed Sacred Writings.

> "That which is conducive to the regeneration of the world and the salvation of the peoples and kindreds of the earth hath been sent down from the heaven of the utterance of Him Who is the Desire of the world. Give ye a hearing ear to the counsels of the Pen of Glory. Better is this for you than all that is on the earth."[61]

Because it is not sufficient to merely imbibe or read the wisdom, which is codified in Sacred Writings, the spiritual seeker must digest that wisdom for themselves, must gain their own personal insight into what it means for their life. This process provides essential elements for that soul's desired transformation. The seeker is even told that they may ask for help to achieve this.

> "Beseech the peerless and incomparable Lord to bestow a penetrating insight upon His servants, for insight leadeth to true knowledge and is conducive to salvation."[62]

Lest wishful thinking lead anyone into assuming that salvation is a one-time occurrence, Sacred Writings make it clear that the process in which souls are engaged is a continuous and never-ending process of refinement of faculties and higher quality experiences, passing through endless territories which are referred to as worlds of God.

> "Suffer this servant, I beseech Thee, to attain unto that which is the cause of his salvation in every world of Thy worlds. Thou art, verily, the Almighty, the Most Powerful, the All-Knowing, the All-Wise."[63]

The human body is mortal and fated to die when the integrated elements which compose it begin to disintegrate, to break down and cease to function. No soul can escape the dissolution of the body with which it is associated; but each soul *can escape fear* of annihilation, fear of its own extinction. Each soul can attain ultimate *liberty from suffering*, can escape mortality, by remembering its inherent immortality. As Bahá'ís see it, this is the vital message brought from age to age by the Manifestation of God for that age. Bahá'ís are those who see in Bahá'u'lláh one who suffered every form of persecution to bring that eternal message once again.

> "The Ancient Beauty hath consented to be bound with chains that mankind may be released from its bondage, and hath accepted to be made a prisoner within this most mighty Stronghold that the whole world may attain unto true liberty."[64]

Whether we fear extinction at the end of this mortal life, or fear the deprivations, exploitations, and persecutions that some humans inflict on other humans during this life, the meaning of salvation from all threats is the attainment of true liberty from all fears.

> "The Bird of the Realm of Utterance voiceth continually this call: 'All things have I willed for thee, and thee, too,

for thine own sake.' If the learned and worldly-wise men of this age were to allow mankind to inhale the fragrance of fellowship and love, every understanding heart would apprehend the meaning of true liberty, and discover the secret of undisturbed peace and absolute composure."[65]

But the purpose of spiritual transformation is only partially fulfilled when an individual grows some noble qualities, communes in adoration, is saved from fears of suffering, and attains true liberty by redeeming or exchanging its old experience of a mortal self for a new and lasting sense of its immortal self – profound as those achievements are. Lest we think that individual salvation is the complete answer to WHY, the higher purpose of transformation and its importance will prove to be greater still.

To Spiritualize Civilization

Individually, the awakening soul begins to notice that it lives in a garden of weeds, an economy of exploitation, and a governance structure that prolongs social injustice. The history of spiritual teachings on this planet reveals a gradually expanding awareness that spirit has the power to transform these injustices by ensuring that every soul becomes increasingly more just in its choices and actions.

Increasingly, the soul experiences dissonance between the new harmony it is feeling within and the crude hostility it is finding around itself. The soul observes that human culture in the material world is not reflecting adequately the symphony of orderliness which the soul has found in its spiritual world. Thus, the soul becomes motivated to reconcile this clash of conditions by cultivating the garden, bringing equity to economic activity, and social justice to the self-management of its settlements, cities, and countries.

By performing this kind of work, the soul finds satisfaction knowing that it is serving its Lord by helping to bring this world into alignment with principles of the higher realm – a sentiment sometimes expressed in the phrases "as above, so below" and "the kingdom of God on earth." So material and spiritual realms begin to merge, bringing into synthesis the greatest achievements of Eastern and Western civilizations.

> "But the honour of the human kingdom is the attainment of spiritual happiness in the human world, the acquisition of the knowledge and love of God. The honour allotted to man is the acquisition of the supreme virtues of the human world. This is his real happiness and felicity. But if material happiness and spiritual felicity be conjoined, it will be 'delight upon delight', as the Arabs say. We pray that God will unite the East and the West in order that these two civilizations may be exchanged and mutually enjoyed."[66]

As the soul develops, it expands the range of its service to others, to society, to humanity, according to the inherent abilities and capacities with which it was born. But the farthest horizons of human fulfillment in service to others, still do not reach the ultimate reason that spiritual development of the soul is important. Beyond all possible human implications and satisfactions, the Creator Itself seems to be waiting for the awakening of each soul.

To Solace the Eyes of the Creator

Here we come upon a great mystery among all the mysteries of creation. The divine Entity is the source from which have sprung all created things. Were It to withdraw Its remembrance of creation, then instantly all creation would cease to exist. By definition, It is an Entity which is self-subsisting and independent of all things. If all of the foregoing statements are true, then it is incomprehensible to us that It still entertains desires, even yearnings, and these desires can be solaced and these yearnings satisfied by something

WHY IS SUCH TRANSFORMATION SO ALL-IMPORTANT?

referred to as Its good-pleasure! These are astounding thoughts. How can It be perfect, transcendent—and still hungry? We *know* that It hungers because It tells us so in numerous ways:

> "HE Who is your Lord, the All-Merciful, cherisheth in His heart the desire of beholding the entire human race as one soul and one body."[67]

> "Make mention of me on My earth, that in My heaven I may remember thee; Thus, shall thine eyes and Mine be solaced."[68]

> "I desire communion with thee, but thou wouldst put no trust in Me. The sword of thy rebellion hath felled the tree of thy hope. At all times I am near unto thee, but thou art ever far from Me. Imperishable glory I have chosen for thee, yet boundless shame thou hast chosen for thyself. While there is yet time, return, and lose not thy chance."[69]

Surely we are hearing a voice rather like the master-puppeteer (Geppetto) who earnestly longed for his favorite invention (Pinocchio) to cease being merely a marionette and instead become "a real boy." We can perceive within our human selves an inherent, moral sense of choice, a capacity to choose and un-choose, an ability to exercise detachment or attachment and thus evolve ourselves within our own limitations. We are admonished to freely make these choices to fulfil the desires of the transcendent Entity that put us into motion that we should achieve our own well-being. Unless and until we accomplish this, we ourselves will feel no satisfaction. It seems that Its desires and ours are inextricably merged, as we hear in the following assertion:

> "There is no peace for thee save by renouncing thyself and turning unto Me; for it behooveth thee to glory in

My name, not in thine own; to put thy trust in Me and not in thyself, since I desire to be loved alone and above all that is."[70]

Divine Love is the mutual attraction holding us in exquisite immersion in Whatever It is. It seems that Its good pleasure is to see us humans finally achieving our complete salvation in joyful reunion.

"Walk ye in the ways of the good pleasure of the Friend and know that His pleasure is in the pleasure of His creatures."[71]

So great is the soul's own joyful pleasure in the heaven of knowledge and nearness, that it desires to see all other human beings (who are equally beloved by God) enjoying the same flights of ecstacy into the heavens of nearness to the Friend. For this reason, intoxicated souls are willing to sacrifice
their own worldly comfort for the sake of others.

"I am he, O my God, who hath embraced Thy love and accepted all the adversities which the world can inflict, who hath offered up himself as a ransom for the sake of Thy loved ones, that they may ascend into the heavens of Thy knowledge and be drawn nearer unto Thee, and may soar in the atmosphere of Thy love and Thy good-pleasure."[72]

Yet, even knowing the glorious outcomes to be achieved, and humbled by the sacrificial assistance being offered, looking at the world, one might conclude that not every soul is ready or able to enter into the process of transformation. So one has to ask, if not now, then WHEN – under what circumstances – can it happen?

CHAPTER 4

WHEN Can Soul Progress Occur?

What Conditions Promote or Prevent It?

Since progressive unfoldment of the soul is of paramount importance to itself, to humanity, and to the Source of its being, then the urgent question becomes, WHEN can such developments occur? What conditions will promote it? And is there anything that might prevent it?

In one sense, soul progress is always possible. As long as there is life, there is hope; because the divine is always present, providing the revelation that guides transformation. However, since humans are endowed with free will, they can turn away from even the greatest of gifts; and in that process turn away from their own noble qualities. We will see that one condition in particular is essential to the soul's development; and the absence of this quality will make further progress impossible. Furthermore, there is a special time in life – its conclusion – when the soul detaches from association with the body that great advancement can occur. And finally, we will find answers that describe further progress that is possible after the body can no longer restrain the soul's expansion.

In One Sense, Transformation Is Always Possible

There is nothing more unlikely than life itself. And yet here we are. The essence of Being, the essence of Reality expresses itself in our being here to marvel at It. And our experience of marveling seems to be related to the original purpose of all existence. "It" The divine Essence seems to have established human consciousness so that It could tell us about Itself. We call this self-expression Its revelation of the nature of Reality. And there is no end to what It has to say. That is what keeps our consciousness expanding and evolving.

> "Among the bounties of God is revelation. Hence revelation is progressive and continuous. It never ceases. It is necessary that the reality of Divinity with all its perfections and attributes should become resplendent in the human world. The reality of Divinity is like an endless ocean. Revelation may be likened to the rain. Can you imagine the cessation of rain? ...the world of existence is continuously progressing and developing; and therefore, assuredly, the virtues characterizing the maturity of man must, likewise, expand and grow."[73]

The daily opportunity for a soul to develop is exactly that: an opportunity – not a guarantee of any kind. For the rational soul has been empowered to make choices and find its own way forward, but *only* to the extent that it will seek and follow divine guidance, thus allowing itself be transformed into a godly creature. This same teaching was espoused in the time of Lord Jesus by the Apostle Paul in his letter to the Romans.

> "Therefore, my brothers, I implore you by God's mercy to offer your very selves to him: a living sacrifice, dedicated and fit for his acceptance, for such is the worship which

you, as rational creatures, should offer. Adapt yourselves no longer to the pattern of this present world, but *let your minds be remade* and your nature thus transformed. Then you will be able to discern the will of God, and to know what is good, acceptable, and perfect."[74] [Emphasis added by the writer.]

The Condition of Truthfulness Is an Absolute Prerequisite

It seemed to the journalist that to "remake" our minds and thus "transform" our nature as Paul urges us to do, would require some intense self-reflection and dissolution of shadowy veils of self-deception. For it is not the lack of truthfulness toward *others* that is our most serious problem. Our most serious problem is the lack of radical transparency and truthfulness within ourselves. Truthfulness is what will enable us to transform our entire reality – both *figure and field*. For we are evolving both the definition of the figure of our "self" and the definition of the place in Reality that we inhabit.

Upon reviewing some relevant passages of revelation, this attribute of truthfulness appeared to be so essential that its absence would bring personal development and success to a *halt*. Truthfulness, it seems, was identified as the "sine qua non", "that without which—nothing" else can happen.

> "Truthfulness is the foundation of all human virtues. Without truthfulness progress and success, in all the worlds of God, are impossible for any soul. When this holy attribute is established in man, all the divine qualities will also be acquired."[75]

The journalist marveled that this passage did not say progress and success are "more difficult" or "slower." It says that progress and success are "impossible" without truthfulness.

Of course, clues about the potency of truthfulness will be observed and analyzed by every seeker independently as they advance along their own path of spiritual discovery. For the journalist, the following passage was particularly eye-catching, as it seemed to purport that truthfulness has the power to change four aspects of the reality that a soul experiences: 1) the place a soul inhabits, 2) the definition of its identity, 3) the place of this soul among others, and 4) its final reward in the sight of God Itself

> "It behooveth you to observe truthfulness, whereby your temples shall be adorned, your names uplifted, your stations exalted amidst men, and a mighty recompense assured for you before God."[76]

While the journalist assembled one possible set of interpretations for these clues as described below, the reader is of course invited to interpret the clues as seems sensible to them. Here is what the journalist noted during contemplation of the passage above:

The passage begins by speaking to souls about "your temples." Now whether you imagine your "temple" as an ashram, a chalet, a hermit's cave, or your own walking and waking "psyche" – it would seem your "temple" is the placeless place in which you live. It travels with you. It is the atmosphere you carry around you, the first impression you give to strangers. It is the composure to which you welcome others when you greet them on the street. This is your spiritual temple. And it says that truthfulness will "adorn" your temple.

Your "name" is the definition of yourself, your complete set of attributes, your signature vibration in all the worlds of God. Truthfulness will be the means to continuously uplift your defining "name." It is the means to leave hypocrisy behind and move toward integrity, into congruence among your perceptions, your thoughts, your speech and actions. Truthfulness will progressively bring harmony to all aspects of your name and "uplift" it.

Your "station" among your peers may be established by the degree to which your internal truthfulness has caused you to become worthy of their trust—someone whose word is the guarantee of their behaviour, someone who is internally unified. As your soul becomes more truthful within itself, it becomes more trustworthy to others. Perhaps in this way it becomes more visible, "more exalted amidst men."

Regarding the "recompense" aspect of the foregoing quotation, the concept is already well known within folk wisdom which states: "what goes around, comes around." As the soul creates truthfulness within itself, it automatically radiates trustworthiness from itself out into the universe; and given enough time (after all, we do have eternity) that "trust" generated in the world eventually comes back upon the soul like an incoming tide. As God is God, It is the keeper of the universe, and watching over all, sees the radiance of personal goodness circle back upon the sender in a mighty *recompense* with mathematical exactitude and certainty. For as the soul progressively trusts itself, it is increasingly able to trust the goodwill encoded in the universe for its benefit, by the Creator of all.

> "Verily it [trustworthiness] is the door of security for all that dwell on earth and a token of glory on the part of the All-Merciful. He who partaketh thereof hath indeed partaken of the treasures of wealth and prosperity. Trustworthiness is the greatest portal leading unto the tranquility and security of the people. In truth the stability of every affair hath depended and doth depend upon it.[77]

Since every affair involves agreements and cooperation, then the trustworthiness of every party to an enterprise is essential. If even one person fails to fulfil what they promised, then the undertaking will not succeed as planned. Trustworthiness works like the guarantor of every contractual agreement. So essential is this quality to the recompense of every enterprise, and the prosperity of every undertaking, that it is even portrayed as a personification of the divine, when the prophetic voice states: I am Trustworthiness.

> "I am Trustworthiness…I will recompense whosoever will cleave unto Me…and hold fast unto My hem. I am the most great ornament of the people…and the vesture of glory unto all who are in the kingdom of creation. I am the supreme instrument for the prosperity of the world, and the horizon of assurance unto all beings."[78]

Gradually each soul becomes further enhanced with attributes such as trustworthiness, prosperity, and assurance as it progressively practices the virtue of truthfulness. Facing truthfully the condition and suffering of others, the soul naturally becomes more kindly, courteous, and forbearing.

> "Say: Let truthfulness and courtesy be your adorning. Suffer not yourselves to be deprived of the robe of forbearance and justice, that the sweet savors of holiness may be wafted from your hearts upon all created things."[79]

These interpretations of the forgoing clues suggest a subtle, and perhaps unexpected, mystical relationship between a soul's capacity for truthfulness and its nearness to God. Since truth is about knowing, and reality is about being, then the more closely one approaches absolute Truth, the closer one reaches to absolute Reality, and that is the ultimate, divine Being. So Bahá'u'lláh advocates to the divine, on behalf of humanity:

> "We beseech Him — exalted be He — to aid everyone to become the essence of truthfulness, and to draw nigh unto Him."[80]

By cultivating radical, radiant, transcendent truthfulness, souls from every human culture find their way through the realms of reality, setting their feet on the most reliable path that leads most directly to their goal – and thus are accounted as finding the "straight" path.

> "O servants! Verily I say, he is to be accounted as truthful who hath beheld the straight Path. That Path is one, and God hath chosen and prepared it. It shineth as resplendent amongst all paths as the sun amongst the stars. Whosoever hath not attained it hath failed to apprehend the truth and hath gone astray. Such are the counsels of the incomparable, the peerless Lord.[81]

Via truthfulness, the soul can progressively dissolve material delusion and thus find its Self standing securely in spiritual Reality. Then when the door opens to expansion, the soul is ready and eager.

Expansion at the Time of Separation from the Body

An exceptional opportunity for expansion of the soul's awareness comes at the time of its separation from associating with the body.

Innumerable studies have documented widespread anecdotes about "near death" experiences – which should perhaps be more accurately referred to as "return from death" experiences. Returnees usually recount a time when their body stopped functioning and they viewed it at a distance, often observing paramedics or first responders trying to call them back into their body. The reason so many returnees give for their protesting "why did you bring me back?" is that they *also* recount an exhilarating experience of "expansion." More than merely rising or flying, many report an explosion outward of awareness, bringing extreme sensations of joy and gratitude. Contemporary documentation of such anecdotal and scientific studies are interesting in their own right.

But we are here, at this stage of the interview, to inquire from Sacred Writings, what can be known of teachings concerning the soul's potential experience during and following cessation of the physical body with which it has been associated. The following passage may be a good place to start as it speaks of a soul preparing itself for departure by sanctifying itself from worldly attachments—and makes the process sound exceedingly attractive.

> "Blessed is the soul which, at the hour of its separation from the body, is sanctified from the vain imaginings of the peoples of the world…If any man be told that which hath been ordained for such a soul in the worlds of God…his whole being will instantly blaze out in his great longing to attain that most exalted, that sanctified and resplendent station."[82]

While we may think of the historical Great Ones, the , as come to advance human culture collectively, they also offer individual souls the understanding needed to prepare for opportunities of expansion at the time of separation from the body, that such souls may become channels of light to the world, responsible for assisting peoples of the world to advance.

> "The Prophets and Messengers of God have been sent down for the sole purpose…to educate all men, that they may, at the hour of death, ascend, in the utmost purity and sanctity and with absolute detachment, to the throne of the Most High. The light which these souls radiate is responsible for the progress of the world and the advancement of its peoples…These souls and symbols of detachment have provided, and will continue to provide, the supreme moving impulse in the world of being."[83]

But after that initial experience of exultation, the soul may begin to recognize that it is still far from ultimate realms of divine being, from the refinement of nearness that it yearns to experience. It will then seek for more progress toward its fulfillment.

Continuous Progress after Dissolution of the Body

An image comes to mind of a human projectile that, having escaped the downward pull of earth, heads out into space, and finding no resistance, continues on in its expanding awareness. So unfathomable is this future that Revelation is unable to convey it to human understanding.

> "Know thou of a truth that the soul, after its separation from the body, will continue to progress until it attaineth the presence of God, in a state and condition which neither the revolution of ages and centuries, nor the changes and chances of this world, can alter. It will endure as long as the Kingdom of God, His sovereignty, His dominion and power will endure. It will manifest the signs of God and His attributes, and will reveal His loving kindness and bounty. The movement of My Pen is stilled when it attempteth to befittingly describe the loftiness and glory of so exalted a station."[84]

While Sacred Writings paint the worlds to come as beautiful, they are also far from boring or predictable. They seem to be full of wonders that are expansive beyond our most glorious hopes.

> "Wert thou to attain unto this station, thou wouldst find wondrous worlds; discover heavenly bowers, celestial gardens, and transcendent realms; and unravel the secrets of the progress of the souls of men through the atmosphere of eternal holiness and the heavens of imperishable glory.[85]

Regarding the continuation of soul progress, it seems according to the following passage, that even the most non-believing souls can be awakened to a better understanding when given assistance. The first line of assistance is by the grace of God.

> "It is even possible for those who have died in sin and unbelief to be transformed, that is, to become the object of divine forgiveness. This is through the grace of God and not through His justice, for grace is to bestow without desert, and justice is to give that which is deserved."[86]

The second line of assistance is from their peers, their friends, their family who still reside in this world. Those who still live in this world have the power to be like wind in the sails of those souls whose progress in the worlds to come may have become like a sailboat becalmed. We have the power to call upon the winds of God to get them moving and progressing again.

> "As the spirit of man lives forever after casting off this elemental frame, it is, like all existing things, undoubtedly capable of progress, and thus one may pray for a departed soul to advance, to be forgiven, or to be made the recipient of divine favours, bounties, and grace."[87]

The third line of assistance is by our own souls even after departing the material world, since revelation says that souls retain the ability to pray for themselves, as well as for that of other souls.

> "As we have the power to pray for those souls here, so too will we have the same power in the next world, the world of the Kingdom. Are not all the creatures in that world the creation of God? They must therefore be able to progress in that world as well... Thus, as souls can progress

WHEN CAN SOUL PROGRESS OCCUR?

in this world through their entreaties and supplications, or through the prayers of holy souls, so too after death can they progress through their own prayers and supplications, particularly if they become the object of the intercession of the holy Manifestations."[88]

By asking WHEN souls can transform, we have received several answers.

First, it is clear that *every moment* can be a moment when the soul can stretch toward new wisdom and greater understanding. So long as truthfulness is guiding the soul's quest, and trustworthiness is manifesting in its behaviour, every moment offers the opportunity to advance further under the influence of divine teachings, thereby making the way more visible to others.

Secondly, at the hour of separation from the body, Sacred Writings assure us all that the soul can experience an unimagined expansion which will benefit both itself and the world in which it has left behind a small body. Such promise makes clear why souls are able to anticipate the arrival of death as a "messenger of joy."[89]

Thirdly, in the unlimited expanses beyond material life associated with a material body. This process of soul unfoldment apparently has no end in sight as it expands into ever greater understanding of the divine, developing likeness to the divine in the qualities and characteristics it manifests. Even death has lost its sting as the soul continues its journey onward to the source of its being.

Evidently, the spiritual experience of soul progress becomes ever more charming as each new realization, by definition, transcends or goes beyond the previous one – thereby expanding and enriching the soul's awareness.

And lest soul transformation be underestimated as merely wishful thinking, we can seek assurance by asking the next question of WHERE evidence of it is to be found?

CHAPTER 5

WHERE Will You Find Evidence of Spiritual Progress?

There is a natural congruence and unity to all expects of human experience – so much so that they unfold in a unified process. What begin as *perceptions* of the world around, form into *thoughts* which may express as *speech*, and then quickly turn into *action*. The sequence of *perception, thought, speech,* and *action* demonstrates how inner and outer aspects of human experience are naturally unified as one continuous phenomenon. Soul development thus shows itself as transformation of both inner spiritual experience and outer social behaviour.

Like all great spiritual paths, Bahá'í Sacred Writings teach the process for redemption and salvation of individual souls. Additionally, Bahá'í Sacred Writings often refer to the collective soul of humanity, its norms, culture, society, civilization and long-range destiny. So, to answer the question of *where* spiritual transformation takes place, we have to look through a matrix-shaped window for evidence of changes both individually and collectively, both outwardly and inwardly.

Inwardly and Outwardly, Individually and Collectively

Suppose for a moment that you have been propelled to the moon and are now looking back upon the earth with eyes like the Designer of worlds, seeing the chaos of human behaviour. When you first look down, you see humans harming each other and their environment because their perceiving and thinking is so murky and confused. You would want to see something drastic happen to light up their inner perceptions and thoughts so that their outer behaviour would become enlightened. If the Designer of worlds were to project a Manifestation of its wisdom into the visible world to talk to humans, the purpose would be to cause an inner enlightenment leading to improvement in outward behaviour. Otherwise, what would be the point of sending such a Manifestation? Bahá'u'lláh poses this very question.

> "And yet, is not the object of every Revelation to effect a transformation in the whole character of mankind, a transformation that shall manifest itself both outwardly and inwardly, that shall affect both its inner life and external conditions? For if the character of mankind be not changed, the futility of God's universal Manifestations would be apparent."[90]

Perhaps it would be inappropriate to laugh at a statement from Sacred Writings, but the use of "futility" above, always makes me chuckle. It is as though the divine is asking Itself, "What's the point?"

Now, due to the existence of human free will, not every human being would respond favorably to a new revelation. But some portion of humanity would listen and respond to divine teachings, would become the source of assistance to their neighbours, and would demonstrate their trustworthiness as trustees of their world. Only such a grand purpose would make it worthwhile for the Designer to emanate a Prophet to the people of earth. Otherwise, it would indeed be pointless for a Prophet to endure the inevitable persecution that comes with a radical new vision if it were to produce no positive change in humankind.

Rather than a futile exercise, the projection of a universal Manifestation to the people of this world successfully finds souls who are prepared to respond eagerly to a Revelation of fresh vision and guidance. The new vision causes these souls to arise as a new people, and undertake a new way of life. These self-identified individuals are referred to as the "people of God" who in turn desire to share the fresh vision and guidance for the betterment of the world.

> "They who are the people of God have no ambition except to revive the world, to ennoble its life, and regenerate its peoples. Truthfulness and goodwill have at all times, marked their relations with all men. Their outward conduct is but a reflection of their inward life, and their inward life a mirror of their outward conduct."[91]

Evidence Is Found Where Inward, Personal Qualities Are Developed

Working backwards from observed behaviour, it becomes clear that outer improvements in quality of action could not manifest except through a preceding improvement to inner thoughts and character.

'Abdu'l-Bahá admonished Bahá'ís concerning inner qualities that would lead to noble conduct and so distinguish them among souls not yet touched by the Revelation of Bahá'u'lláh. He illustrated this with 14 qualities in particular from a myriad of possible virtues. These qualities are identified below in italics by the author.

> "Should any one of you enter a city, he should become a center of *attraction* by reason of his *sincerity*, his *faithfulness* and *love*, his *honesty* and *fidelity*, his *truthfulness* and *loving-kindness* towards all the peoples of the world, so that the people of that city may cry out and say: 'This man is unquestionably a Bahá'í, for his *manners*, his *behaviour*, his *conduct*, his *morals*, his *nature* and *disposition* reflect the attributes of the Bahá'ís.'"[92]

We can safely assume that 'Abdu'l-Bahá does not waste words or repeat himself needlessly. So, it was interesting to look more closely at the implications of each one of those attributes. No shadow of deception or dissimulation could hide among the radiant qualities of *sincerity, honesty,* and *truthfulness*. No whim or fickleness would ever tarnish or weaken relationship with a person who exhibited only *faithfulness* and *fidelity*. And no harm would ever come from a person whose responds to everyone with *loving-kindness*.

These initial qualities then were related to dimensions of action that might follow from them such as: *manners* or the general outward bearing that people display; *behaviour* toward themselves and others; *conduct* as the ways in which they direct or manage their affairs; *morals* as the rightness and justness of choices they make; *nature* as the most fundamental of their innate qualities; and *disposition* as the prevailing moods and temperament that colour their every moment.

Evidence Is Found Where Outward Personal Behaviours Are Refined

Concurrently, the process of continuous, internal, spiritual transcendence leads an individual to improve their behaviour and personal achievements, moving toward excellence in all aspects of their art of living, creating a life that integrates personal development in service to others. Because spiritual unfoldment has no final limit, there is also no limit to a life of continuous, refreshing improvements in personal behaviour.

In the following excerpt, 'Abdu'l-Bahá calls attention to the need for refinement of personal behaviour so that souls achieving this can then become channels for "holiness." What seems so potent in the statement is an assertion that by refining one's character, manners and conduct, one may serve to "quicken the dead" in the sense of awakening and educating others to respond to the Manifestation of God whose purpose is to bring all souls to recognize their spiritual reality.

> "The most vital duty, in this day, is to purify your characters, to correct your manners, and improve your conduct. The beloved of the Merciful must show forth such character and conduct among His creatures, that the fragrance of their holiness may be shed upon the whole world, and may quicken the dead, inasmuch as the purpose of the Manifestation of God and the dawning of the limitless lights of the Invisible is to educate the souls of men, and refine the character of every living man—so that blessed individuals, who have freed themselves from the murk of the animal world, shall rise up with those qualities which are the adornings of the reality of man.[93]

The phrases "educating souls" and "refining character" sound like extended processes requiring time to develop the inherent potential of a human being into a more refined outer behaviour. And those qualities finally evidenced in their behaviour are enhancements or "adornings" not of some feeble *hope* for nobility, but rather of revealing the essential, inalienable noble *reality* of each person which has been waiting to be developed and brought to light.

Behaving with righteousness, with "rectitude of conduct," leads directly to discovering that one's identity is universal. All of humankind are made of one and the same material, the same perceiving heart. This shared identity is eternal; the differences are material and finite and therefore will be no more.

> "It is incumbent upon everyone to show the utmost love, rectitude of conduct, straightforwardness, and sincere kindliness unto all the peoples and kindreds of the world, be they friends or strangers. So intense must be the spirit of love and loving kindness, that the stranger may find himself a friend, the enemy a true brother, no difference whatsoever existing between them. For universality is of God and all limitations earthly."[94]

Writings suggest that a developing soul recognizes its own need for encouragement, and realizes that other souls also need support to keep striving toward their own highest accomplishment as spiritual beings. In a world of corruption and hypocrisy, everyone is called once again to purity so that they may become buttressed to express continuously their inner spiritual progress as powerful outward action.

> "…They must be constantly encouraged and made eager to gain all the summits of human accomplishment, so that from their earliest years they will be taught to have high aims, to conduct themselves well, to be chaste, pure, and undefiled, and will learn to be of powerful resolve and firm of purpose in all things…"[95]

In speaking especially with regard to youth, Shoghi Effendi, unequaled in his immersion in Sacred Writings, highlighted one inner quality that would be especially inspiring to others at the conclusion of the Second World War – and that was optimism, *joyous optimism* about the future of humanity. Such historical confidence could only have its origin in the certitude felt by living a life that is congruent in its expression: from purity within, to exemplary outward conduct toward others.

> "...Above all, they should set a high example...chastity, politeness, friendliness, hospitality, joyous optimism about the ultimate future happiness and well-being of mankind, should distinguish them and win over to them the love and admiration of their fellow youth. The thing which is most conspicuously lacking in modern life is a high standard of conduct and good character; the young Bahá'ís must demonstrate both, if they hope to seriously win over to the Faith members of their own generation, so sorely disillusioned and so contaminated by the laxity war gives rise to."[96]

Finally, to guide personal behaviour, a new definition is introduced concerning "freedom from prejudice" that goes far beyond merely accepting diversities of economic class, ethnicity, colour, citizenship, creed, height, age, and weight – all qualities that are irrelevant to equality and nobility. The definition sets a new standard for *freedom from prejudice* when it urges all to enter every consultation with "an open receptive mind" that has "renounced all preconceived ideas."

> "If five people meet together to seek for truth, they must begin by cutting themselves free from all their own special conditions and renouncing all preconceived ideas. In order to find truth, we must give up our prejudices, our own small trivial notions; an open receptive mind is

essential. If our chalice is full of self, there is no room in it for the water of life. The fact that we imagine ourselves to be right and everybody else wrong is the greatest of all obstacles in the path towards unity, and unity is necessary if we would reach truth, for truth is one."[97]

The capacity to consult toward refinement and unity of thought, is what creates the bridge to societal transformation. Searching for truth together leads people to identify common values; and this in turn enables them to coordinate their activities and collaborate to improve their society.

Evidence Is Found Where Inward Cultural Values of a Society Are Improved

During his extended tour of Western Europe and North America in 1912, 'Abdu'l-Bahá was acutely aware of the cultural values he was encountering in societies immersed in materialism and growing industrial power. He foresaw their competition in power leading inexorably toward a violent contest between states. Consequently, he used public events throughout these regions to articulate how their inner collective values would determine their historical path.

He reminded people of the obvious: that a nation's "culture" is what cultivates the values of that society, and determines the quality of "civilization" or lawfulness which that society will follow. A society bent on material power for its own sake would lionize those people who achieve material power; and a society dedicated to advancing human dignity would admire those people who promote a divinely inspired civilization. He saw scientific advancement and material progress as natural outcomes of human intelligence that could produce either malignant or beneficial results depending upon the aspirations that guided them. Technical advancements would benefit humankind only when inspired and guided by divine ideals for human dignity.

"Material civilization concerns the world of matter or bodies, but divine civilization is the realm of ethics and moralities. Until the moral degree of the nations is advanced, and human virtues attain a lofty level, happiness for mankind is impossible." [98]

Since his pronouncement, world events continue to demonstrate that failure to align the design of technologies with spiritual civilization leads to destruction of societies rather than advancement in human well-being.

"...all these weapons of war are the malignant fruits of material civilization. Had material civilization been combined with divine civilization, these fiery weapons would never have been invented." [99]

A society establishing laws and conditions to promote human advancement is what the Great Ones came to establish.

"The divine civilization is good because it cultivates morals. Consider what the Prophets of God have contributed to human morality. Jesus Christ summoned all to the Most Great Peace through the acquisition of pure morals."[100]

From age to age, Divine Educators have renewed cultural values that result in the elevation of humanity through the dynamic cohesion of material and spiritual aspects of civilization.

"Christ ratified and proclaimed the foundation of the law of Moses. Muḥammad and all the Prophets have revoiced that same foundation of reality. Therefore, the purposes and accomplishments of the divine Messengers have been one and the same. They were the source of advancement to the body politic and the cause of the honor and divine civilization of humanity, the foundation of which is one and the same in every dispensation.[101]

To help them understand how the *collective soul of a society* is cultivated and developed, 'Abdu'l-Bahá provided his audiences with examples that they could see in their own public lives. He referred to the magnetic power of commonly held values as "collective centres" –meaning cultural value centres that could bond people into a collective force. The examples He provides are formatted individually below for the reader's consideration.

"In the contingent world there are many collective centers which are conducive to association and unity between the children of men. For example:

- patriotism is a collective center,
- nationalism is a collective center,
- identity of interests is a collective center,
- political alliance is a collective center,
- the union of ideals is a collective center,

and the prosperity of the world of humanity is dependent upon the organization and promotion of the collective centers. [However], with the appearance of great revolutions and upheavals, all these collective centers are swept away."[102]

He was emphasizing two important conclusions about social values that become collective centres of social development. The first conclusion was that human society relies on such common values for its effective organization and resulting prosperity. The truth of this is obvious. Human well-being is completely dependent upon the voluntary cooperation of individual people with socially-adopted guidelines or rules of behaviour. For example, a non-smoking zone is violated if just one person lights up; a pandemic quarantine is violated if just one infected person enters the area; organic agriculture is violated if just one neighbour uses air-borne pesticides. There are no second chances, no exceptions. It's a voluntary covenant with a social value. As he says, "the prosperity of the world of humanity is dependent upon…promotion of…collective centers."

But his second conclusion is even more significant. When humans invent an ideology, whether that be about nation, labour union, political approach, or social movements, other humans can just as easily sweep away that ideology with revolutions of their own making. This is the ephemeral nature of popular trends and social movements when they are tied to the changeable nature of anything less than the reality of eternal principles.

Eternal principles are transcendent of history. They are unchangeable. They are axiomatic – realities so self-evident that you could list them yourself: human beings did not create the cosmos; human beings are all formed of the same substance; actions have consequences that react upon the actor; and so on. What is common to these axiomatic statements is that they testify to an ultimate unity of human nature, welfare, and fulfilment.

Throughout the long history of human cultures, the greatest proponents of these eternal principles have been exceptional Figures who become the Divine Educators of humanity, unveiling previously unsuspected aspects of eternal Reality and providing contemporary guidance in the form of laws and institutions prescribed for the betterment of the historical times in which they appeared. The vision they propounded is of a humanity living in ultimate harmony with itself, unified in its conduct by a "kingdom" of universally admired laws and social institutions.

> "…the Collective Center of the Kingdom, embodying the institutions and divine teachings, is the eternal **Collective** Center. It establishes relationship between the East and the West, organizes the oneness of the world of humanity, and destroys the foundation of differences. It overcomes and includes all the other collective centers."[103]

Evidence Is Found Where a Society Is Outwardly Progressing in Its Social Justice

Among the most powerful of eternal principles to advance human society are those of justice and equity. Justice provides each thing and every actor with the conditions required by its essential nature to flourish. Justice for a cactus is to receive just a little water; while for a lotus, it is to be submerged in water. Justice for one who kills may be a lifetime in prison, while for another it may be a medal of honour.

> "Justice and equity are twin Guardians that watch over men. From them are revealed such blessed and perspicuous words as are the cause of the well-being of the world and the protection of the nations."[104]

Justice provides a consequence perfectly matched to the action. Equity ensures that adjustments perfectly suit the individuals involved such as rewarding fairly both capitalists and labourers, or again, rewarding appropriately those nations that provide raw materials and those that manufacture them. In this way, we see inner cultural values begin to manifest as outer societal practices.

Societies do not seem to advance in a straight line of progress. When materialism and mortal-thinking dominate social consciousness, you can observe a decline in societal norms. Conversely, to the degree that awareness of spiritual reality and unending life of human souls dominate social consciousness, then societies are able to make true progress in social justice and human well-being.

> "In the world of spirit there is no retrogression. The world of mortality is a world of contradictions, of opposites; motion being compulsory everything must either go

forward or retreat. In the realm of spirit there is no retreat possible, all movement is bound to be towards a perfect state. "Progress" is the expression of spirit in the world of matter."[105]

In the most practical terms, the expansion of spiritual values in a culture leads to outwardly observable progress even in the most mundane aspects of society such as its economic life.

"The fundamentals of the whole economic condition are divine in nature and are associated with the world of the heart and spirit. This is fully explained in the Bahá'í teaching, and without knowledge of its principles no improvement in the economic state can be realized… When the love of God is established, everything else will be realized. This is the true foundation of all economics. Reflect upon it."[106]

In his popular addresses, 'Abdu'l-Bahá provided his audiences with numerous examples of how throughout history societies have responded visibly when their collective inner vision is spiritualized. He offered an example that all audiences in Europe and North America would recognize.

"…**Moses** was appointed for their deliverance and training. He guided them, led them out of bondage into the Holy Land, uplifted them from ignorance and despair, trained them so that they rose from a condition of lowliness and subjection into one of honor and importance, and enabled them to reach a high degree of perfection. They became proficient in sciences and arts, attained a lofty plane of civilization, honorable and esteemed among nations, whereas formerly they had been lowly and despised. They were ignorant; they became intelligent, finally reaching that period of supremacy and power witnessed in the Solomonic sovereignty. Their name became widespread throughout the world, and they were esteemed for distinct virtues."[107]

Similarly, he reminded Christians in the audience that Christ had drawn people of all ethnicities and nations into unity with each other in dedication to their common faith, and that this resulted in the elevation of their societies.

> "…For example, **Christ** educated and developed mankind universally. He rescued nations and peoples from the bondage of superstition and idolatry. He summoned them all to the knowledge of the oneness of God. They were dark, they became illumined; they were material, they became spiritual; earthly they were, they became heavenly. He enlightened the world of morality."[108]

The Qu'rán acknowledges the transformative influence of Moses upon his people, and of Christ assembling many ethnicities into one common faith. Similarly, the prophetic figure of Muhammad was able to unite warring Arab tribes into a single nation of elevated culture.

> "**Muhammad** appeared as a Prophet among such a people. He educated these barbarous tribes, lifted them out of their ignorance and savagery and put an end to the continuous strife and hatred which had existed among them. He established agreement and reconciliation among them, unified them and taught them to look upon each other as brothers. Through His training they advanced rapidly in prestige and civilization. They were formerly ignorant; they became wise. They were barbarous; they attained refinement and culture. They were debased and

brutal; He uplifted and elevated them. They were humiliated and despised; their civilization and renown spread throughout the world."[109]

With his own eyes, Abdu'l-Baha had seen the transformative effect of the revelations of Bahá'u'lláh upon the peoples of Persia, not to mention those among whom Bahá'u'lláh ministered during the years of His many exiles in the region. The consequence of transforming inner cultural values, was to make a shared commitment to serving the rest of humanity from the abundance of spiritual insights they enjoyed – even when those new social attributes forced waves of Bahá'ís out of their homeland into a diaspora around the world.

"**Bahá'u'lláh** appeared in Persia at a time when the darkness of ignorance enveloped the East, and there was no trace of human love and fellowship… He so refined the souls of the Persians who followed Him that they attained a station of highest intelligence and reflected the attributes of perfection to the world. Whereas formerly they were ignorant, they became knowing; they were weak, they became mighty; they were without integrity, they became conscientious; they were hostile toward all men, they developed love for humanity; they were spiritually negligent, they became mindful and attentive; they were sleeping, they became awakened; they disagreed among themselves, they united in love and are now striving to render service to the world of humankind."[110]

So dramatic is the evidence of spiritual transformation both inwardly and outwardly, both individually and collectively, that a conscientious seeker is eager to understand HOW is all this possible? It will become evident that a seeking soul can promote their own advancement through acquiring knowledge, making decisions with their free will, and undertaking actions that benefit themselves and society.

But before launching into HOW soul development is accomplished, the journalist requires a time out to reflect on how the first set of answers illustrate a new vision of FAITH.

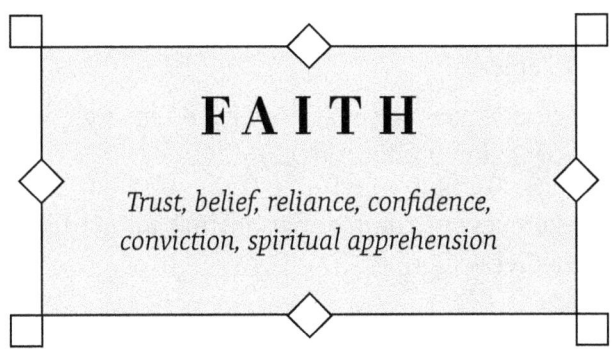

FAITH

Trust, belief, reliance, confidence, conviction, spiritual apprehension

Almost by definition, an investigative journalist does not know in advance how a given interview will unfold, or what it will discover. When this interview began, the journalist merely wanted to discover how the mysteries of spiritual transcendence could be demystified into recognizable daily language. The classic series of questions began with: WHO, WHAT, WHY, WHEN, and WHERE? So, it came as a surprise when the answers to these questions began to throw a whole new light on the realm of faith.

Previously, the journalist held connotations of Faith clustered around those concepts above, along with acceptance and assurance of the truth of *Something*. Often, that something was a vague sense of whatever God is – but since "It" is ultimately beyond human names for attributes, definition, and designations – the resulting "faith" was quite amorphous and formless.

Suddenly, the interview had began to describe with clarity some other focal points of faith:

WHO: each human Soul is…

- Endowed with thought and wisdom, to discern the truth in things and understand
- Able to seek intelligently and draw its own conclusions, by investigation and research;

- Capable of benefiting the world, inspiring both arts and sciences to emerge;
- Paradoxically, moving yet still; a mysterious sign of the nature of God in both worlds.

WHAT: the process of transformation that unfolds each soul's potential involves…

- Profound personal purification of actions, speech, thoughts and even perceptions;
- Noticing the magnetic attraction of divine Love;
- Rotating to align to that attraction; moving toward it; and
- Assimilating into the attraction of Love by detachment from former things.

WHY: astounding outcomes motivating soul development include…

- To develop noble qualities in the soul
- To be educated by all creation – fulfilling its purpose
- To fulfil the soul's unique capacity to know and love its Creator
- To attain a new kind of expanding salvation
- To spiritualize their society creating a new civilization
- To solace the eyes of the Creator, watching the soul come forth

WHEN: the times and conditions that either promote or prevent a soul developing include…

- Potentially, always, since divine revelation is always present to educate the soul;
- When souls are engaged in trying to apply divine guidance;

- When Truthfulness is present, souls can advance; but not in its absence;
- When Trustworthiness it present, it enables one soul to assist other souls to advance;
- At the time of its death, when freedom from the body allows for soul expansion; and
- In the eternal realm where souls continue to advance through prayerful yearning.

WHERE: the places where soul unfoldment displays evidence encompass...

- Within the person's spiritual consciousness
- Without, in the person's observable behaviors
- Within the collective, cultural values of a society
- Without, in a society's equity and justice in its laws and practices

The interviewer is taken aback by the clarity with which their simple questions have elicited such highly defined answers about the nature of souls and the importance of their development.

So far, the answers have been in the form of assertions about the potential of souls and their destined development. Seeing is truly believing. Therefore, each soul needs to experience these "truths" directly to know for itself that they are true.

But, HOW?

CHAPTER 6

HOW Does *Knowledge* Prepare Souls to Transform?

Our journalist friend has been interviewing God about the mysteries of spiritual transformation—trying to de-mystify the process of transformation into operations an engineer could appreciate. The initial questions already answered include: **Who** is the soul? **What** is transformation? **Why** is it so important? **When** does it occur - under what conditions? and **Where** would you find the effects of transformation if and when it does occur?

At this point, the engineer in us wants the journalist to pose the most pragmatic question of all: *how* does transformation occur? Specifically, what initiates the process? What sustains it? And what completes it? Fortunately, there is *a remarkably clear formula* that applies to constructive processes across the entire spectrum of human enterprise. The formula is: knowledge + volition + action.

> "The attainment of any object is conditioned upon knowledge**,** volition and action**.** Unless these three conditions are forthcoming, there is no execution or accomplishment. In the erection of a house, it is first necessary to know the ground, and design the house suitable for it; second, to obtain the means or funds necessary for the construction; third, actually to build it."[111]

From the simple metaphor of house construction to the far more subtle process of improving the level of justice in society, the same formula still applies.

> "Mere knowledge of principles is not sufficient. We all know and admit that justice is good, but there is need of volition and action to...manifest it."[112]

Imagine removing any one of these elements from the process, and you'll find evidence that all three are required simultaneously for success. Any effort, that uses only two of the three elements, will prove futile.

For example, strong will power and furious action might force some kind of result, but the effects would probably not be good if knowledge were missing about what is efficient, effective and beneficial.

Likewise, one could have adequate knowledge of how to do many things and take action to start many projects, but if volition were weak or wavering, these projects would be lacking in perseverance and might well be left unfinished.

Then there is the dreamer who has adequate knowledge and volition (as desire) to picture any number of projects, but lacking action, these projects remain at the idea stage only.

The balance of this chapter will focus on knowledge as an essential element for any constructive process asking: What is it? How is it developed? And, how does it mature? We will ask about knowledge, both in itself – and in relation to action. We will ask about how knowledge is developed using three distinctive domains of education. And finally, we will ask what it means for knowledge to mature – as all living things mature.

Knowledge Is Required for Why and How to Act

Having established the interdependence of knowledge, volition, and action, we now focus attention on the element of knowledge.

HOW DOES KNOWLEDGE PREPARE SOULS TO TRANSFORM?

To say that knowledge is a good thing seems an obvious truism. But not *all* knowledge is good. And of that which is good, not all knowledge is equal. For example, knowledge of *how* to take action, may be less critical to real success than knowledge of *why* to take action – and the consequences that action may have to benefit or harm humanity.

In this deeper look into the value of knowledge, we discover that knowledge is much more than merely *instrumental* to the achieving of good deeds. It can also provide the deep, moral context of action. For example, the "knowledge of God" implies an admiration and adoration of the cosmos, the planet, and the people who consciously inhabit it. This knowledge and appreciation generates a spiritual love and sincere desire to care for people and planet – thereby guiding and enhancing actions to achieve their highest outcome.

> "...Briefly, good deeds become perfect and complete *only* after the knowledge of God has been acquired... Otherwise, though good deeds be praiseworthy, if they do not spring from the knowledge of God, from the love of God, and from a sincere intention, they will be imperfect... In like manner, while those who perform good deeds are to be lauded, if these deeds do not flow from the knowledge and love of God, they are assuredly imperfect."[113]

If an agent of good deeds acts mechanically, going through the motions, they will be as though sleepwalking. To perform good deeds unconsciously is like a lamp that has no awareness it is lighting a room; or a beast of burden that trudges along only to be fed, not knowing it is bringing medicine to a remote clinic. Such mechanical, or animal agents neither learn new spiritual skills, nor critique the efficiency of their act, neither expand their awareness of the recipients of this action, nor evaluate the impact and effectiveness of their action. For the human agent who is unconscious of their doings, nothing has really happened. They receive no benefit of expanded understanding or vision from their labour.

With this focus on awareness, 'Abdu'l-Bahá sets a higher standard than merely ethical actions that are mechanically performed. The standard is awareness. Conscious knowledge must be achieved *prior* to an ethical action before it can truly be called a spiritual act.

Knowledge Is a Treasure in the Soul

We humans live our days in a material universe where everything is finite, mutable, and subject to deterioration. Even we ourselves are connected to a physical body that is mortal. But the divine teachings guide us to seek that knowledge which leads to everlasting life as the following passage indicates:

> "...that which leads to everlasting life, eternal honour, universal enlightenment, and true success and salvation is, first and foremost, the knowledge of God. It is clear that this knowledge takes precedence over every other knowledge and constitutes the greatest virtue of the human world."[114]

Knowledge of God is that which leads to everlasting life of the soul and endures within it is as the greatest virtue for the soul to attain.

Our attraction to knowledge is a transcendent process – meaning that with every new insight and understanding, we find ourselves wanting the next, and the next, always seeking to transcend one state of knowledge into the next higher, broader and more encompassing state. So it is that all forms of knowledge eventually lead us to the pursuit of spiritual knowledge.

> "Knowledge is as wings to man's life, and a ladder for his ascent... In truth, knowledge is a veritable treasure for

HOW DOES KNOWLEDGE PREPARE SOULS TO TRANSFORM?

man, and a source of glory, of bounty, of joy, of exaltation, of cheer and gladness unto him."[115]

As happens to the increasing number of astronauts who return intoxicated from space having seen our blue pearl of a planet floating within a thin veil of atmosphere in the emptiness of sterile space, subtle, spiritual knowledge lifts us into a state of ecstacy. Our own sense of self is engulfed in something much larger, grander, and more glorious. Spiritual knowledge is an indisputable treasure; and we are ennobled by being the "treasury" entrusted to hold and preserve such treasure. The deeper the mystery, the more we are concerned to cherish it and not casually display it before those who are unprepared to assess its value. Bahá'u'lláh enjoins us with the following:

> "Ye are My treasury, for in you I have treasured the pearls of My in and the gems of My knowledge. Guard them from the strangers amidst My servants and from the ungodly amongst My people."[116]

All people belong to Him; this includes those agnostics who are unsure about a divine being, and those atheists who have definitely chosen to be "ungodly" in the sense of acknowledging no transcendent Being, and seeking no divine guidance. Others, who are already god-fearing and wish to be servants to a higher Cause, may yet be far removed from approaching higher understanding and so in that sense be "strangers" to finer knowledge. So it achieves nothing for one acquainted with a mystery to try to impart it to one who has yet to experience it for themselves. Each soul has a unique path into transcendent mysteries, and cannot appropriate the direct knowledge of a different soul.

Yet, the way is open for each and every soul to explore extensively, explore without limit, as each human being has latent within them the capacity to "pattern recognize" whatever exists.

"Patterns" would include entities and attributes of entities for example which are referred to as "names"—meaning attributes—of the unseen Source from which they emerged. For those who espouse "knowledge creation" as either individual naming of a new concept, or social construction of knowledge, then this process can be thought of as the human "naming" of something that has not been recognized before. A *figure* emerges out of a sparkle-dust *field* of relativity because a human being endows it with a name.

> "Now, the world of existence, indeed every created thing, proclaims but one of the names of God, but the reality of man is an all-encompassing and universal reality which is the seat of the revelation of all the divine perfections. That is, a sign of each one of the names, attributes, and perfections that we ascribe to God exists in man. If such were not the case, he would be unable to imagine and comprehend these perfections."[117]

The most reliable and expansive knowledge is to be found in both the life-book and the written-book of a Manifestation of God, those rare Beings who appear on earth to restore humanity in periods of history when divine inspiration has declined among the people. Yet so often when a Manifestation appears, their divine nature is neither understood nor appreciated – and the masses of people flee from the very thing they have been yearning for, as attested by the life of Bahá'u'lláh.

> "The Book of God hath been sent down in the form of this Youth... Take ye good heed, O peoples of the world, lest ye flee from His face... He it is Who hath created you; He it is Who hath nourished your souls...and enabled you to recognize Him Who is the Almighty, the Most Exalted, the All-Knowing. He it is Who hath unveiled to your eyes

the treasures of His knowledge, and caused you to ascend unto the heaven of certitude —the certitude of His resistless, His irrefutable, and most exalted Faith."[118]

We see that the greatest and best of all knowledge resides with the Manifestations of God who come from age to age to enlighten humanity. These Manifestations exist on earth for only a short period; and leave behind only a small number who were willing to learn from Their revelation. The ones who have learned from revelation realize that human intelligence alone can never reach such heights and so recognize the necessity of knowledge-sharing through systematic education.

Intelligence & Talents Need Education

Let us look further into the idea that all the names or attributes of God can be mirrored or reflected, recognized or known by a human being. This potential for complete knowledge leads to the idea mentioned earlier of each person being a treasury within which divine mysteries have been entrusted. So it is that a human being can serve as a talisman - a container—into which have been trusted primordial truths that lead us toward understanding our own essence. The Arabic word for a charm is *tilsam* which can in turn be traced to the ancient Greek verb *telein* which means "to initiate into the mysteries."[119] These mysteries lead to an ultimate end of searching (*telos*) which is knowledge of our own essence. However, the point can be made that just as a seed may germinate better with good cultivation, inchoate knowledge can become conscious knowledge more effectively when enabled by good educational practices - and without them, human potential may unfortunately remain under-developed.

"Man is the supreme Talisman. Lack of a proper education hath, however, deprived him of that which he doth inherently possess...The Great Being saith: Regard man as a mine rich in gems of inestimable value. Education can, alone, cause it to reveal its treasures, and enable mankind to benefit therefrom."[120]

To awaken conscious knowledge from inherent knowledge will require some skillful exploration – and that's where we discover the need for an exploration guide, an "educator" – one who will lead ("duco") the seeker out of ("ex") their unawareness, into the light of awareness. To appreciate the value of *true* education, we have to free ourselves from any unfortunate thoughts regarding the current state of practice when it comes to education in our societies today. Instead, we can indulge ourselves in thoughts of what an ideal set of educational practices would look like when carried out with skill.

Ideal Education Is of Three Distinct Kinds

It helps us to imagine an ideal education if we begin with awareness of three realms of knowledge. Each of these realms is an essential aspect of human life – our physical health (requiring food, sleep, and activity), our social well-being (requiring economic and political organization), and our spiritual progress (requiring awareness of the human soul and its development through the guidance of Divine Educators). It's that final form of education and knowledge that we will carry us out of this world into life beyond.

> "...education is of three kinds: material, human, and spiritual.
>
> **Material education** aims at the progress and development of the body, through gaining its sustenance, its material comfort and ease. This education is common to animals and man.

> **Human education**, however, consists in civilization and progress, that is, sound governance, social order, human welfare, commerce and industry, arts and sciences, momentous discoveries, and great undertakings, which are the central features distinguishing man from the animal.
>
> As to **divine education**, it is the education of the Kingdom and consists in acquiring divine perfections. This is indeed true education, for by its virtue man becomes the focal centre of divine blessings and the embodiment of the verse "Let Us make man in Our image, after Our likeness." This is the ultimate goal of the world of humanity."[121]

So complex and comprehensive is the range of education required to develop human potential, it is inconceivable that masses of people could accomplish this for themselves unaided. Even the autodidact – the self-conducted learner – searches out expert assistance. Traditional knowledge transmission characteristically relied upon an almost intimate relationship between a "knowledge holder" and members of the following generations. Such qualitatively deep learning would of necessity involve small numbers.

However, ensuring the true educational development of masses of people will require some form of systemic overview. Designing a national framework for education would require addressing both common and specialized aspects of education tailored to suit that nation. It would also be necessary to follow up such initial design with effective coordination of its implementation. Perhaps we should be evaluating nations not on their highly unequal distribution of GDP (Gross Domestic Product) but rather on the successful cultivation of their entire citizenship through GDE (General Development by Education). An abundance of national benefits would follow, such as: increased productivity and creativity, improved health and longevity, reduced violence and crime, and perhaps even elevated participation in international forums of science and arts. What could be more pivotal to a nation's stature in the world?

> "The primary, the most urgent requirement is the promotion of education. It is inconceivable that any nation should achieve prosperity and success unless this paramount, this fundamental concern is carried forward."[122]

As with the macro-level of national development, so it is at the micro-level of each individual life. A person of any age who wishes to improve themselves and the quality of their life, must seek out the education that best suits their intelligence, talents and circumstances. When a person does this, their commitment to refining themselves and the world, is accepted God as *worship*, an offering of their life's endeavours. Writing to a young student, 'Abdu'l-Bahá made this point to them, that as God is the essence of knowledge and beauty, then serving those entities is serving God.

> "Thus, as thou enterest a school of agriculture and strivest in the acquisition of that science thou art day and night engaged in acts of worship—acts that are accepted at the threshold of the Almighty. What bounty greater than this that science should be considered as an act of worship and art as service to the Kingdom of God."[123]

The converse of educational development is for a person to become the blind imitator of previous generations. Their life becomes a mechanical repetition of family history, each day an unthinking routine. Not only do they themselves not advance in understanding but they fail to add to their family's pool of knowledge, and they fail to contribute to the improvement of society.

> "Those who are uninformed of the world of reality, who do not comprehend existing things, who are without perception of the inner truth of creation, who do not penetrate

HOW DOES KNOWLEDGE PREPARE SOULS TO TRANSFORM?

the real mysteries of material and spiritual phenomena and who possess only a superficial idea of universal life and being, are but embodiments of pure ignorance. They believe only that which they have heard from their fathers and ancestors. Of themselves they have no hearing, no sight, no reason, no intellect; they rely solely upon tradition."[124]

This of course does not denigrate all traditional knowledge or customs. As there is wisdom and insight in every culture, each generation therein may create practices to carry forward that wisdom into a different time. But that is exactly the point: each generation must look with fresh eyes at the traditional statements, customs, and practices they have inherited and evaluate them by asking: Does this traditional practice still carry wisdom applicable to the new circumstances our generation is facing? Can we go forward with this practice, or should we discard it as anachronous and burdensome to our culture; and instead *refresh* our traditions with a new custom suitable to our times?"

By adopting this approach to the transformation and renewal of traditions, each generation makes its unique contribution to cultivating society and civilization.

"God has given us eyes, that we may look about us at the world, and lay hold of whatsoever will further civilization and the arts of living." [125]

To examine culture with fresh eyes, looking for what to remove and what to add, will take great discernment and wisdom.

Wisdom Guides the Use of Knowledge and Its Expression in Speech

The expanse of human knowledge is like an endless array of specialized tools. The function of wisdom is to determine exactly which tool is *best suited to a given circumstance*, as defined by the time, the place, and the one who will apply that new knowledge and those who will see it expressed or applied. We have already addressed the fact that certain knowledge from direct experience of divine mysteries can never, ever be expressed. Furthermore...

> "...'Not everything that a man knoweth can be disclosed, nor can everything that he can disclose be regarded as timely, nor can every timely utterance be considered as suited to the capacity of those who hear it.' Such is the consummate wisdom to be observed in thy pursuits. Be not oblivious thereof, if thou wishest to be a man of action under all conditions. First diagnose the disease and identify the malady, then prescribe the remedy, for such is the perfect method of the skilful physician."[126]

"Suitability to those who hear it", implies not only selecting the most relevant knowledge content, but also expressing that knowledge with qualities of heart that are sensitive and beneficial to the recipient.

> "Even so, this activity should be tempered with wisdom—not that wisdom which requireth one to be silent and forgetful of such an obligation—but rather that which requireth one to display divine tolerance, love, kindness, patience, a goodly character, and holy deeds."[127]

There is a larger context to the wise use of knowledge than the strictly personal or even inter-personal context; and that is suitability to the society around and the unfolding conduct of world affairs. When we pray for assistance to gain knowledge from the divine repository, that request may be self-centred and not be suitable to the well-being of others. In which case, the request for assistance may be denied out of divine wisdom.

HOW DOES KNOWLEDGE PREPARE SOULS TO TRANSFORM?

> "But [at times] we ask for things which the divine wisdom does not desire for us, and there is no answer to our prayer. His wisdom does not sanction what we wish. We pray, "O God! Make me wealthy!" If this prayer were universally answered, human affairs would be at a standstill… The affairs of the world would be interfered with, energies crippled, and progress hindered. But whatever we ask for which is in accord with divine wisdom, God will answer. Assuredly!"[128]

A further wisdom regarding right use of knowledge is that it should conform to ultimate Truth (an epistemological concept) and therefore properly allude to Reality (an ontological concept). It is evident that the standard of error-free knowledge is expressed through the consummate wisdom of the Prophets of God. It is their divine Mission to educate the whole of humanity toward unity and well-being.

> "…That is, since the essential infallibility of the universal Manifestations of God has been established, whatsoever proceeds from Them is identical with the truth and conformable to reality."[129]

The knowledge of so-called learned men is as nothing when compared with the Knowledge of universal Manifestations, as described below:

> "Their so-called learning, when compared with that Knowledge, is utter falsehood, and all their understanding naught but blatant error. Nay, whatsoever proceedeth from these Mines of divine Wisdom and these Treasuries of eternal knowledge is truth, and naught else but the truth. The saying: *"Knowledge is one point, which the foolish have multiplied"* is a proof of Our argument, and the

tradition: "*Knowledge is a light which God sheddeth into the heart of whomsoever He willeth*" a confirmation of Our statement."[130]

The wisest of all purveyors of knowledge are therefore the great Educators, those Manifestations of the divine, who come to share with humanity that knowledge which is the true expression of reality. Their mission is to dispel confounding falsehoods, so that all humanity may re-align itself to the source of all being.

"The Prophets of God have been inspired with the message of love and unity. The Books of God have been revealed for the upbuilding of fellowship and union. The Prophets of God have been the servants of reality; Their teachings constitute the science of reality. Reality is one; it does not admit plurality. We conclude, therefore, that the foundation of the religions of God is one foundation." [131]

Every One of them conveys the same true knowledge, about the same eternal reality, showing us, from age to age, the same straight and most direct path homeward. For this service, we revere Them, and set Them before all our endeavours to know and understand, as the very standard of wisdom.

To follow Them, learn from Them, grow in character and strength through Their guidance, is our only hope for authentic personal and societal advancement. But choosing to follow Them, means not choosing other attractions and ways of living. This is the dilemma of human free will and volition. When we are prey to unhealthy habits and ignorance, how can our human **volition** release us to choose again?

CHAPTER 7

HOW Does *Volition* Free Souls to Transform?

The exercise of human volition, or will-power, is actually not about *power* at all, in the sense of force. Rather, volition is about *choices*, about being "willing" to do one thing and not another. We will ask for details about this defining characteristic of human souls—contrasting it with other forms of will.

At times, "free-will" has been used to mean any old choice, in any old direction—as though freedom implied randomness and equal value to every choice. While the exercise of such unguided freedom would open innumerable options, those options would *not* be equal to each other, since they will not yield equal benefit for the person making the choice or for others experiencing the consequences of that choice. Therefore, our question here can better be rephrased to ask: which choices, freely made, will assist the seeker in their pursuit of spiritual transformation?—remembering that every active choice means *not choosing* other options.

If we want to join those who seek to advance spiritually, to become something new and better, the implications are obvious: we will have to make choices to relinquish some ways we used to live; leave behind some worlds we thought we lived in; and let go of some identities we thought we were. As Jesus said, *"You ought not to be astonished…when I tell you that you must be born over again.*"[132] So how do we get our human volition to release us again and again from any places we have been stuck in our process of transforming?

Several fascinating aspects of human volition will be considered in this chapter. An obvious starting point is to contrast human will with the harmonious, niche-specific behaviours of other creatures populating nature.

A second contrast will be highlighted between the opportunities to make choices that are found here in this material world and those in the worlds to come. With regard to important choices that we make in this world, it will be alarming to notice that will power can become paralyzed by certain conditions that resemble spiritual illnesses. But it will also be reassuring to discover that will power is actually learned, and can improve with practice.

We will reflect on why the highest development of human will is alignment with Divine Will; and discover that when this beneficial alignment occurs, human will power can become supercharged by divine confirmations thereby making ordinary human beings capable of heroic and saintly acts.

Additional comparisons will help to develop a context for understanding human volition. We will review some Sacred Writings concerning volition of the Creator, of the Manifestations, and of the perfect exemplar of submission or servitude, 'Abdu'l-Bahá.

Let's begin by contrasting human free will with niche-specific behaviours found in nature.

How Humans Escape the Niche-Specific Behaviours in Nature

With regard to volition, it is clear that rivers flow downhill; they cannot choose otherwise. With regard to migration, fish and reindeer may seek another route if their migration is frustrated; but neither can choose to fly. Flight is not part of their niche.

HOW DOES VOLITION FREE SOULS TO TRANSFORM?

Their behaviour operates within the niche they occupy in nature – which is water for fish, and land for reindeer. The human being alone can escape their initial niche.

Thus, the ability to innovate beyond any one niche and live in all environments of planet earth, and even beyond it, is evidence of a volition in human beings that is beyond any other creature found in nature. The freedom of choice that humans enjoy is aided by their ability to generalize from specific observations, make inferences about connections, and predict future occurrences – all of which result from abstractions and ideations that are removed from direct, sensory experience.

> "Nature is without volition and acts perforce, whereas man possesses a mighty will...it is evident that man is more noble and superior; that in him there is an ideal power surpassing nature."[133]

Even when a human being misuses their free will and runs afoul of consequences that harm themselves or others, they are still empowered to use their volition to self-correct and...

> "...can voluntarily discontinue vices; nature has no power to modify the influence of its instincts." [134]

With regard to what could be called "natural gifts" in a human being, their inborn talents and abilities, these do not come ready-made for use upon adulthood. Human beings have to develop those innate gifts through education, practice, perseverance, and the exercise of their personal volition.

> "Unto each one hath been prescribed a pre-ordained measure, as decreed in God's mighty and guarded Tablets. All that which ye potentially possess can, however, be manifested only as a result of your own volition."[135]

Each soul has both the capacity and the responsibility to manifest divine virtues or "perfections."

It can achieve this by training its free will to align with divine Will; and training itself to desire what God desires for the benefit of that soul.

> "I implore Thee, O my Lord, by Thy name, the splendors of which have encompassed the earth and the heavens, to enable me so to surrender my will to what Thou hast decreed in Thy Tablets, that I may cease to discover within me any desire except what Thou didst desire through the power of Thy sovereignty, and any will save what Thou didst destine for me by Thy will."[136]

Choices the Soul Can Make in This World and the Next

A second intriguing aspect of human volition, or the free will of the soul, is to be found in how it may be used in this world and the next. We may have assumed that whether we use will power for self-development this year or not, there isn't really any rush. We may think we have "all the time in the world." And as we begin to assume we actually will live forever, we may think that we can exercise free will any time in the coming eternal continuum. But this assumption may not be valid; it may be that personal volition is of a distinctive kind in this world and the same opportunity is *not open* in the worlds to come. What do you make of the reference below to "the degree of purity" attained by a soul during its life in the physical world? And what does it mean "to remain in the ocean of God's Mercy?"

> "As to the soul of man after death, it remains in the degree of purity to which it has evolved during life in the physical body, and after it is freed from the body it remains plunged in the ocean of God's Mercy. From the moment

HOW DOES VOLITION FREE SOULS TO TRANSFORM?

the soul leaves the body and arrives in the Heavenly World, its evolution is spiritual, and that evolution is: the approaching unto God."[137]

This contrast between worlds is a mysterious question, which will certainly have to wait until we gain direct experience of the worlds to come and the forms of volition that we have there. But the quotation appears to say that an individual is capable of making critical choices and qualitative changes to purify their life and identity while here, associated with their physical body, in a world of materiality and mortality. For example, it's only possible to be generous in this world of scarcity; an individual cannot be generous in a world with no limitations on resources. Again, it's only possible to be courageous is this world where your body can die; an individual cannot be courageous in a world where nobody dies. This material world of shadows offers so many opportunities to develop heavenly virtues, before it's too late.

The choices one makes here create sensations as though moving from the depths of an ocean, where the specific gravity is very dense, and gradually striving upward into lighter and lighter concentrations; or in spiritual terms, purifying one's thoughts and behaviours toward spiritual identity.

Again, in this world, one can make qualitative choices about moving upward in the same way a pilot chooses to climb higher during take-off toward the final cruise altitude. This is what the soul seems to be doing until released from association with the body. Then, the degree of purity to which it has attained, becomes fixed in some sense as its cruising altitude.

At least we are assured by the preceding quotation that the degree of purity can never be degraded because the soul "remains" in that degree of purity. Furthermore, the soul's evolution is never-ending, in the sense that it "remains plunged in the ocean of God's Mercy." In that realm, the soul begins to make a kind of advance toward the presence of God, drawn forward by its *yearning* for nearness, propelled by the *goodwill* of others for its advance, and allowed to approach by the infinite *mercy* of God, removing all barriers such as one's memory of unworthiness.

However, all is not well in this world of opportunities. This precious free-will can become paralyzed.

Potential Paralysis of Volition by Four Spiritual Illnesses

With regard to those critical choices that we make in this world, it's alarming to realize that volition can become paralyzed by certain conditions that resemble spiritual illnesses. This can occur even to those who have been drawn to a Manifestation such as Bahá'u'lláh, who believe in the value of His spiritual teachings and eagerly desire to share them for the enlightenment of others. The soul inspired to uplift society may feel as though it's in a battle against injustice and a crusade to help those in need – but *before* it can be effective, such a soul has to overcome its own tendency to paralysis caused by unfavorable spiritual conditions.

Two such spiritual illnesses are *apathy* (an unwillingness to know) and *lethargy* (an unwillingness to do). The following statement urges those with aspirations to serve, to first overcome any inertia they may feel coming from such conditions.

> "…the apathy and lethargy that paralyze their spiritual faculties…are among the formidable obstacles that stand in the path of every would-be warrior in the service of Bahá'u'lláh, obstacles which he must battle against and surmount in his crusade for the redemption of his own countrymen."[138]

A third spiritual illness that can paralyze human volition is indifference, a lack of compassion for others, making it possible to ignore the urgent suffering of other people. 'Abdu'l-Bahá asks rhetorically, *"Why is man so hard of heart?"* and answers *"It is because he does not yet know God."*[139] As awareness of God deepens in people, so too does the sense that all things are connected, that everything is sacred, and that all people are related to each other, a single race, indeed a single family, even a single entity, living a shared life experience in this world.

A fourth spiritual illness that can paralyze will power is fear of death. Will power is weakened in direct proportion to preoccupation with the material world and the pervasive mortality of everything that lives here. Those who lack awareness of God, eternity, infinity, and continuous life of their soul, can become obsessed with the destined mortality of their own body. This obsession with a dissolution they cannot prevent, then drives them to trivial pursuits in an effort to numb and obscure the fear of death.

> "The conception of annihilation is a factor in human degradation, a cause of human debasement and lowliness, a source of human fear and abjection. It has been conducive to the dispersion and weakening of human thought, whereas the realization of existence and continuity has upraised man to sublimity of ideals, established the foundations of human progress and stimulated the development of heavenly virtues… If he dwells upon the thought of nonexistence, he will become utterly incompetent; with weakened willpower his ambition for progress will be lessened and the acquisition of human virtues will cease."[140]

Fortunately, there is a way to resist and overcome these spiritual illnesses.

How to Practice Aligning Human Will to Divine Will

While it's alarming to realize that human willpower can become paralyzed by apathy, lethargy, indifference or fear of non-existence, it's equally reassuring to discover that willpower is actually learned, can be developed over time, and improved with practice. Parents have a high calling to educate their children in the right use of will power. Beginning in childhood, a little person who is sustained by the love of their parents, can learn to expand their reach and explore the world around them. Over time, they can develop patience and persistence as they try to accomplish more and more difficult tasks and goals. With guidance, young people can grow into powerful individuals able to live with dignity and high resolve, developing stronger and stronger volition lifelong as they go.

> "Thus shall these tender infants be nurtured at the breast of the knowledge of God and His love. Thus shall they grow and flourish, and be taught righteousness and the dignity of humankind, resolution and the will to strive and to endure. Thus shall they learn perseverance in all things, the will to advance, high-mindedness and high resolve, chastity and purity of life. Thus shall they be enabled to carry to a successful conclusion whatsoever they undertake."[141]

When human beings have developed such strong volition as is suggested by "resolution.. the will to strive.. to endure.. perseverance.. the will to advance…and high resolve" it is no wonder that they have the capacity "to carry to a successful conclusion *whatsoever* they undertake." But then how will they decide precisely *what* to undertake with this mighty will of theirs? Wanting the best possible outcomes, they will endeavour to make choices not based on the *wildest* use of their free will, but rather on the *wisest* use of their free will.

Each soul can accomplish wise choices by freely aligning its volition to the direction of divine will, which is the will of its Greatest Well-Wisher. This alignment is sometimes referred to as "submission," but its effect is uplifting as in aligning ones flight to the sustaining lift of a jet stream. Jet streams are bands of strong wind that generally blow from west to east all across the globe and therefore assist flights heading east. Aligning to the direction of divine will is a submission that increasingly frees a human soul from wasteful effort, unwise decisions and harmful consequences.

> "That which beseemeth man is submission unto such restraints as will protect him from his own ignorance, and guard him against the harm of the mischief-maker. Liberty causeth man to overstep the bounds of propriety, and to infringe on the dignity of his station."[142]

The consequence of such beneficial guidance is an unparalleled degree of freedom. Submitting to parameters of wisdom actually accelerates the success that human volition can achieve – rather like a lesser vehicle sliding into the slipstream of a much more powerful vehicle – the effort is less, and the advancements increase. For the apprentice choosing servitude to a master, the initial obedience is what leads to mastery and the greater liberty to achieve that comes with skillfulness.

> "Say: True liberty consisteth in man's submission unto My commandments, little as ye know it. Were men to observe that which We have sent down unto them from the Heaven of Revelation, they would, of a certainty, attain unto perfect liberty… Say: The liberty that profiteth you is to be found nowhere except in complete servitude unto God, the Eternal Truth. Whoso hath tasted of its sweetness will refuse to barter it for all the dominion of earth and heaven."[143]

So then, what happens as a consequence of such alignment?

Divine Alignment Supercharges a Soul's Will Power

When this beneficial alignment is firmly established, human will power can become super-charged by divine confirmations that make ordinary human beings capable of heroic and saintly acts. An example is found in the life of Tahirih, titled Qurratu'l-'Ayn, Solace of the Eyes, a poetess and philosopher in 19th century Iran. Her volition became galvanized and submerged in the divine by her contact with Bahá'u'lláh – a transformation that led to her dramatic appearance, unveiled, in the presence of men at the conference of Badasht.

> "Qurratu'l-'Ayn was a Persian woman without fame and importance—...When she saw Bahá'u'lláh, she changed completely, visibly, and looked within another world. The reins of volition were taken out of her hands by heavenly attraction... She became so attracted to the divine threshold that she forsook everything and went forth to the plain of Bada*sh*t, no fear in her heart, dauntless, intrepid, openly proclaiming the message of light which had come to her."[144]

Whereas previously, her wisdom and poetry had been shared with audiences of men from behind a curtain, at the conference of Badasht, she came forth from her tent without a veil, causing great consternation among some of the men present. and eventually leading to her death. Her fearless devotion to propagating the message of the Báb which was faced with violent opposition throughout society, eventually led to her martyrdom. The volition of Tahirih, totally immersed in divine will, was an example of how human volition can become magnified when confirmed by divine will.

Evidence of the same astonishing transformation of human will was also apparent in the lives of the disciples of Jesus Christ.

> "Consider what Christ accomplished. He caused souls to attain a station where with complete willingness and joy they laid down their lives. What a power! Thousands of human souls, in the utmost joy because of their spiritual susceptibilities, were so attracted to God that they were dispossessed of volition, deprived of will in His path. If they had been told simply that sacrifice in the path of God was good and praiseworthy, this would never have happened. They would not have acted. Christ attracted them, wrested the reins of control from them, and they went forth in ecstasy to sacrifice themselves."[145]

The mystery of sacrifice is that to the outside observer it looks like giving up something as important life itself. But to the insider, seeing already worlds far beyond, and their own endless life in those worlds, the release from this world cannot come soon enough. While only a relative few every come to that degree of sacrifice, the principle holds true for everyone: reaching for the divine, lifts mere humans into the will power of immortals.

Volition of the Creator

This brings us then to wonder about volition of the One Who has such overwhelmingly attractive power as to absorb the volition of human beings *once they have freely expressed their willingness*. Voluntary surrender of will occurs whenever one expresses the sentiment **"…Thy will be done."**[146]

Our focus on divine will and its purpose runs counter to the thoughts of those individuals who assume that God is disinterested in this world or the doings of human beings. The full power of divine volition is evident through the length and breadth of existence. All this and more that we cannot apprehend originated in that Primal Will.

"Thou doest, through the power of Thy might, what Thou willest, and ordainest, by an act of Thy volition, what Thou pleasest. The will of the most resolute of men is as nothing when compared with the compelling evidences of Thy will, and the determination of the most inflexible among Thy creatures is dissipated before the manifold revelations of Thy purpose."[147]

Paradoxically, the absolute dominion of divine will may have been the very motive to bring into being a human creature who could choose to turn away, even though all that souls have, even that free will, originates with God.

"Magnified be Thy name, O Lord my God! Thou art He Whom all things worship and Who worshipeth no one, Who is the Lord of all things and is the vassal of none, Who knoweth all things and is known of none… Thou didst wish to make Thyself known unto men; therefore, Thou didst, through a word of Thy mouth, bring creation into being and fashion the universe… I implore Thee, by this very word that hath shone forth above the horizon of Thy will, to enable me to drink deep of the living waters through which Thou hast vivified the hearts of Thy chosen ones and quickened the souls of them that love Thee…"[148]

Knowing what a struggle it is for humans to align their will to the divine, how much more astonishing is it to observe the complete submission to divine will demonstrated by the Prophets and Manifestations of God.

Volition of the Manifestations

Between the absolute power of divine will and the relative powerlessness of human will there is a gap that cannot logically

HOW DOES VOLITION FREE SOULS TO TRANSFORM?

be bridged from either side. If the absolutely powerful were to impose itself upon the lesser being, it would compromise its own intention to create a little being with free will. Conversely, for the miniscule human being to be able, by its own will, to accomplish entry into the presence of the divine, it would need to become equal to or greater than the divine. Both these foregoing ideas are illogical.

The unbridgeable gap can only be filled by a special-purpose Being, a Prophet as called by some, an Avatar by others, and by still others, a Manifestation or emanation from God that is visible to human beings and can communicate with them. Bahá'í Sacred Writings assert that among such Beings are Abraham, Moses, Jesus, Mohammad, and in this day Bahá'u'lláh. These special purpose Beings are not God, as God cannot be contained within its entire creation, let alone within a mere fragment such as a human body. But Manifestations are able to express divine will through the model of their lives and their Revelations. This they do not of their own will but that of God alone as evidenced by Bahá'u'lláh when He said: *"By My life! Not of Mine own volition have I revealed Myself, but God, of His own choosing, hath manifested Me."* [149]

At times, the voice of God itself speaks through them; sometimes they speak in the voice of a Prophet or even a philosopher. But they also demonstrate the condition of absolute submission to God. This they characterize as the station of a servant – and for them an absolute condition of servitude.

> "And were they to say, **"We are the Servants of God,"** this also is a manifest and indisputable fact. For they have been made manifest in the uttermost state of servitude, a servitude the like of which no man can possibly attain."[150]

Then we find a personage who, though not a prophet, embodies ideal human virtues, and occupies a unique station in spiritual history.

Volition of the Master, 'Abdu'l-Bahá

While human beings, with our imperfections, are unable to replicate the pristine state of submission demonstrated by the Manifestations, we have been offered the example of one exceptional human being. Although unique in his station in all of spiritual history, 'Abdu'l-Bahá yet provided us with an approachable model of an ideal human being, in the same way a master does for an apprentice. For this reason Bahá'ís refer to him with the title of Master, as conferred by Bahá'u'lláh. For himself, he consistently rejected any association of himself with the Manifestation except as a servant. He said he is, as his name translates, the servant of Bahá (Glory).

> "My station is the station of servitude—a servitude, which is complete, pure and real, firmly established, enduring, obvious, explicitly revealed and subject to no interpretation whatever..."[151]

He extended this role of service both to the Manifestation and to almighty God. And he proclaimed that in this role of servitude he found complete fulfilment, satisfaction, ecstacy, and his "Sadratu'l-Muntaha" - the tree which marks the ultimate goal, the terminal point of a journey, his omega.

> " 'Abdu'l-Bahá is himself a servant at the Threshold of the Blessed Beauty and a manifestation of pure and utter servitude at the Threshold of the Almighty. He hath no other station or title, no other rank or power. This is my ultimate Purpose, my eternal Paradise, my holiest Temple and my Sadratu'l-Muntahá."[152]

Through the moments and events of his life, 'Abdu'l-Bahá demonstrated that submitting his will in service to the divine

How Does Volition Free Souls to Transform?

purpose, brought him an alluring and intoxicating experience like the fragrance of jasmine, which caused his soul to blossom, and past sorrow to be consoled.

> "By Thy Power, verily, the sweetness of servitude is the food of my spirit; with the fragrance of servitude my breast will be dilated, my being refreshed, my heart delighted, my eyes brightened, my nostrils perfumed, and in it is the healing of my disease, the allaying of my burning thirst, the soothing of my pain."[153]

'Abdu'l-Bahá revealed that His surrender of personal will in preference for servitude to God, led Him to an elevated condition He describes as a blazing crown and glorious throne. It provided His life a guiding star and equipped Him with a drawn sword to fulfil His purpose. With crystal clarity He portrays that surrender to servitude is His absolute desire beyond which He desires no other condition.

> "This is my station and condition; this is my blazing crown; this is my glorious throne; because my servitude to the Holy Threshold is my brilliant light, my shining star and my drawn sword; and beside this I have no other name."[154]

Returning to Focus on the Soul's Free Will

Having considered volition in the divine Essence, in Its historical Manifestations, and in the unique person of 'Abdu'l-Bahá, we have a much-expanded context in which to view the soul's free will.

In the end, there is nothing simple about human volition and the will that souls can exercise to free themselves of attachment to things of this world. Human souls use their volition to expand beyond the niche-specific behaviours of animals. Souls persevere through this worldly life in a manner some poets describe as a pilgrimage, orienting themselves towards ever-expanding horizons in the worlds to come. After souls are released from association with a physical body, the downward pull of this material world can no longer affect them; and the mercy of God will draw them forward to the degree that they desire it and that they are supported by prayers on their behalf.

We saw that the good intentions which souls may hold, can be thwarted if their volition becomes paralyzed by such spiritual illnesses as apathy, lethargy, indifference, or fear of mortality and extinction. We also saw that developing and exercising willpower begins in childhood, can be cultivated through education, and continues to improve with practice lifelong.

We contemplated why it is that the highest development of human will is alignment with Divine Will. When this beneficial alignment occurs, human will power can become super-charged by divine confirmations making ordinary human beings capable of heroic and saintly acts as demonstrated in the life of Tahirih in the 19th century, and in the lives of spiritually surrendered Christians in the centuries since the ministry of Jesus.

But the willpower of souls has to work upon something – their own condition, or that of others, or on the social conditions that surround them all. Every kind of work is achieved by ACTION that achieves some goal and transforms souls in the process.

CHAPTER 8

HOW does ACTION Produce Transformation?

This question evokes a remarkable sequence of answers, that reach far beyond simply: "Action gets things done."

- Actions develop inner and outer Soul coherence;
- Actions that benefit others also benefit the actor;
- Consistent actions invoke the blessings of perseverance;
- Actions provide the dynamic force of example;
- Action is what gradually transforms the world.

If this world were simply made of imagination, then there would be no need for action…(What?) The kinds of events we usually call "action" (requiring us to move things with muscles, and move people with persuasion) would be entirely unnecessary because the first two elements of transformation (namely knowledge and will) would be enough. We could simply use knowledge to inform our options, and then use willpower to "imagine" one state of being changing into another. Choose, will, imagine, and it would be done.

But this material world in which we find ourselves, does not allow for imagination to be sufficient. Imagination may be a pre-requisite to set life goals, design a building, or plan out a novel;

but imagination alone cannot bring either fiction or fact into being. Even fiction must have an author and a building must actually be built. Imagination has to be followed by action which then brings *coherence* between the inner life of a human being that is visible only to God, and the outer life that is visible to other human beings.

Actions Develop Inner and Outer Soul Coherence

That the inner and the outer life of human beings develop in tandem is the purpose for which every Manifestation comes into the world, bringing divine education and enlightenment to humanity, so that humanity may translate new vision into new action.

> "The purpose of the one true God in manifesting Himself… is to array every man with the mantle of a saintly character, and to adorn him with the ornament of holy and goodly deeds."[155]

Evidently the actions we undertake, or the deeds we perform, are evaluated against two standards: they are evaluated on the degree to which they are "holy" or dedicated to Spirit, and in the humanitarian sense of being more or less "goodly" – meaning beneficial to other beings.

When our outer actions are congruent with the values we inwardly espouse, then the coherence we achieve wins the good pleasure of our highest role model, the person of 'Abdu'l-Bahá, the Master, who wrote to one earnest adherent, *"Praise be to God! You have proved your words by deeds…"*[156] Action is the final proof that the inside and outside of one's life are in harmony.

Actions that Benefit Others Also Benefit the Actor

We do not know the inner condition of those around us. They may be burdened or suffering far more than we know. By living

HOW DOES ACTION PRODUCE TRANSFORMATION?

congruently from within to without, and acting consistently in our commitment to right action at every moment, every day, we may unknowingly bestow a greeting, a kind word, an act of assistance or an expression of appreciation to someone that has far more impact on them than we could have known. Our simple action may even be lifesaving for someone who has lost hope in life, or faith in others. It may bring back their will to go on living.

> "One righteous act…is endowed with a potency that can so elevate the dust as to cause it to pass beyond the heaven of heavens. It can tear every bond asunder, and hath the power to restore the force that hath spent itself and vanished."[157]

We may have preferred to think that our life's work is some grand ambition that will be achieved on some far distant day through heroic action. But what if our life's work consists of the totality of our smallest daily actions? What if the life's work of any of us is really nothing more than the cumulative sum of our deeds day-by-day? It benefits us to reflect on the quality of our deeds since each daily action adds up to the sum of our life, like an abacus. The continuum of daily actions may stop at any moment and none of us knows when that moment will come. We live like a traveler on standby at the airport, never knowing when our call will come. So we must be attentive.

> "Bring thyself to account each day ere thou art summoned to a reckoning; for death, unheralded, shall come upon thee and thou shalt be called to give account for thy deeds."[158]

This daily accounting for the quality of our deeds should not be worrisome or alarming if we are truly endeavouring to live the best we can. We will always fall short of perfections we can imagine. We will always struggle with circumstances to bring things into a better condition. Our obligation is not to achieve (since achievement ultimately is in the hand of God). Our obligation is to be present and to do all things the best we can. We can only give each action our best effort and then pray that some benefit will come from it as we send it out into the world.

What we might *not* anticipate is that, due the cosmic accounting of things, we may one day encounter the very benefit we were trying so hard to bring to others. This is commonly understood in popular discourse as the effect of karma, the cosmic continuity of a force once it is set in motion. The least philosophical of people can be heard to say: "what goes around comes around." In more blessed and elevated language, this cosmic principle is much the same.

> "No goodly deed was or will ever be lost, for benevolent acts are treasures preserved with God for the benefit of those who act. Blessed the servant and the maidservant who have fulfilled their obligation in the path of God our Lord, the Lord of all worlds..."[159]

So realizing that our deeds actually matter a great deal both to others and to ourselves, we may then commit to making our daily actions as consistent with our values of righteousness as we possibly can. An outstanding principle of right actions, recognized in religious traditions worldwide, has been the one known as the golden rule—doing unto others as you would have them do unto you. This rule sets a standard of justice for our actions toward all others equally without prejudice toward any.

What sometimes gets overlooked is the way we treat ourselves. A kind of zealous self-righteousness can overtake a well-meaning actor who then unwittingly short-changes themselves or their family members in the pursuit of serving "humanity." It is enlightening to reflect on the following quotation.

> "Be fair to *yourselves* and to others…that the evidences of justice may be revealed through your deeds among Our faithful servants."[160]

The statement indicates that the universality of justice requires us to think of ourselves neither above others nor below others, but equal (which is the most difficult of all three attitudes to maintain). Equality requires that we treat ourselves as compassionately as we treat others. If we invite others to rest when they are tired, then we should demonstrate such kindness toward ourselves. A pattern of excessive self-sacrifice may be intended to demonstrate righteousness, but then actually demonstrates a lack of consistency and equity. Being consistent in our kindness creates a unity in which we ourselves are not excluded from the rest of humanity.

Consistent Actions Invoke the Blessings of Perseverance

Being consistent across time also brings benefits. Perseverance is defined as the continued effort to do or achieve something despite difficulties, failure, or opposition. In one sense, it is a familiar concept, commonly understood as described in the excerpts below:

> "Everything of importance in this world demands the close attention of its seeker. The one in pursuit of anything must undergo difficulties and hardships until the object in view is attained and the great success is obtained."[161]

> "Perseverance is an essential condition. In every project firmness and steadfastness will undoubtedly lead to good results; otherwise it will exist for some days, and then be discontinued."[162]

Such familiar usages of perseverance tend to focus our attention on the outer project or purpose being focused on. What may go unnoticed is that the term is not really outwardly directed. It is inwardly directed! It is an intransitive verb happening to the *self*, as in: I run; I meditate; I persevere. It is the Self of the soul that is changing through perseverance just as much, or maybe more, than the outer conditions that are being acted upon.

The fact that "to persevere" causes changes within the character of the actor, awakens awareness that character develops as the soul acquires virtuous qualities or what are referred to in Bahá'í Sacred Writings as "divine perfections." A further exploration of these Sacred Writings to see what other virtues are associated with this quality of perseverance, produces a remarkably vivid set of soul qualities, including the following:

- "courage, faith, and perseverance"[163]
- "initiative, resourcefulness, generosity, fidelity and perseverance…"[164]
- "patience, endurance, resolution, and perseverance…"[165]
- "courage…self-abnegation…fortitude and… perseverance."[166]

What you may have noticed with those four clusters of noble qualities is that they are concluded with a final exhortation to "persevere." The sequences makes good sense. If you are already doing the right things, but are still not at your goal, then what's left is for you to "persevere." This logic makes it all the more interesting to find some clusters of heroic qualities in which perseverance is *not* the final exhortation. For example, we find the sequence:

- "…perseverance…determination, firmness of purpose…"[167]

Here you can see the actor constantly engaged with their work, and persevering. But if that is not enough to bring about the desired result, then the actor can intensify their continuity by adding "determination." This humble term "determination" can be underestimated as though it implies only grim, teeth-clenching "grit"—similar to the quality of stubbornness. But "determination" is actually a much more subtle concept than that.

Remember our previous review of the idiom "willpower"? Its meaning was not power as *force* at all, but rather the decisive power of "choice". Now "determination" is similar. It means that the actor is going to *determine* the outcome of their present undertaking. They firmly choose their outcome—their proposed goal - their purpose. And then, accept nothing less. When the soul becomes firm in the only goal it will accept, then it has "determined" without doubt what the outcome of its quest will be. Firmly holding this determination, it can then calmly and gracefully persevere.

Another sequence that amplifies "perseverance" with additional noble qualities is the following:

- "the utmost courage, perseverance, fortitude and self-sacrifice."[168]

In this example, the actor with a courageous heart is persevering in their action, and two more noble qualities are added to it: fortitude and self-sacrifice. Fortitude of course, coming from the French origin, means "strength" - but what kind of strength? It may imply strength of focus, achieved by accepting the given situation and engaging with it, rather than losing focus by wishing this effort weren't needed. Reminds me of a wise general who once said you have to decide to "fight the war you are in, not the war you wish you were in; and fight with the army you've got, not the army you wish you had." That soul shows "fortitude" who decides to accept (not avoid) the challenge it faces and engage with it until the chosen purpose is achieved.

Which brings us to the second quality shown here to amplify courageous perseverance and that is "self-sacrifice." Since the soul-self continues forever, it is technically not possible to sacrifice it. But the ego-self which is identified with the body and biography, has its own likes and dislikes, its own preferences that may try to displace the soul's chosen purpose, and toward which the soul is persevering. When this competition arises, the soul can amplify its perseverance by sacrificing or relinquishing the preferences of the ego-self. So it is that soul-identification increases while ego-identification decreases.

As these inner virtues intensify and reinforce each other, changes to the actor's inner life, become evident in the actor's outwardly observable behaviour; and thus form a clear role model for others to see and perhaps follow.

Actions Provide the Dynamic Force of Example

Personal transformation, as we articulated in an earlier chapter, involves an iterative process of purification, atunement, turning and aligning to the call of divine love, then moving into heavenly attachments that detach the soul from former things. As the transformation process advances, everyday deeds become congruent with heavenly values and model a path for others that can lead them toward their own transcendent fulfilment.

> "Pass beyond the *narrow* retreats of your evil and corrupt desires, and advance into the *vast immensity* of the realm of God, and abide ye in the meads of sanctity and of detachment, that the fragrance of your deeds may *lead the whole of mankind* to the ocean of God's unfading glory."[169]

Conversely, if deeds fail to match words then the power to model a path for others is lost.

> "…Beware…lest ye walk in the ways of them whose words differ from their deeds…Let your acts *be a guide unto all mankind*, for the professions of most men, be they high or low, differ from their conduct. It is through your deeds that ye can distinguish yourselves from others."[170]

Action moves outward from thought, first benefitting the actor by virtuous changes within, then to becoming a model for others through the force of example, and finally radiating onward into the world.

Ultimately, It Is Action that Gradually Transforms the World

It's really quite simple. The wrong in the world is not intractable. It *can* be corrected. Whether injustices in the world are environmental or social, they can all be reversed, and better conditions achieved, by taking the appropriate actions.

> "The betterment of the world…can be accomplished through pure and goodly deeds, through commendable and seemly conduct."[171]

This latter term "conduct" points to a concept of management as in "the conduct of my daily affairs", or "the way we conduct our operations." It is broader than any one discrete action or deed; it is a whole consistent pattern of behavior such that there is no turning back to weak, inadequate or corrupt former patterns.

If betterment of the world is achieved through goodly deeds, then the converse is equally true. The stagnation of the world, in a degraded state of material contamination or social injustice, takes its momentum from the inaction of those who, seeing what could be better, wait for someone else to do it.

> "The wrong in the world continues to exist just because people talk only of their ideals, and do not strive to put them into practice. If actions took the place of words, the world's misery would very soon be changed into comfort."[172]

Lest we become discouraged or demoralized by the vastness of worldly wrongs that need correcting, we can remind ourselves of the unfathomable impact of even one goodly deed. As we saw before with "one righteous act", even one virtuous deed, undertaken in a context of darkness or hopelessness, shines in a way that can fundamentally alter that place.

A single goodly action proves that evil is not absolute; goodness is present; and if goodness is present, it can prevail. Goodness can overcome; goodness can triumph; and a world once dominated by darkness, will become illumined by heavenly possibilities.

"One holy action maketh the world of earth highest paradise."[173]

But of ourselves, having nothing, being nothing, we cannot bring any undertaking to completion. All actions are animated by a spiritual dynamic that we did not originate. That spiritual dynamic is "divine grace"—toward which we direct the final question of this interview.

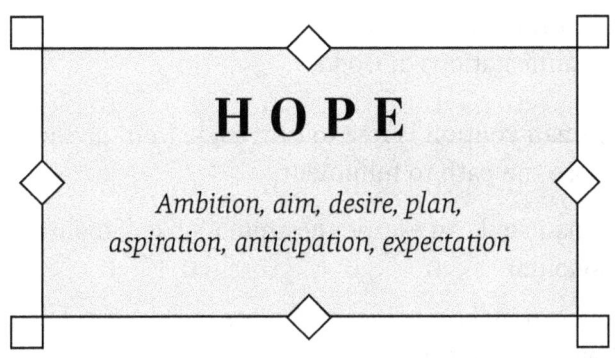

HOPE

Ambition, aim, desire, plan, aspiration, anticipation, expectation

In reviewing notes pertaining to the three factors which 'Abdu'l-Bahá identified as essential for anything to be accomplished – including soul development—the journalist infers that a soul having the **ambition** and **desire** to expand and progress, can galvanize that **aspiration** with progressively more profound knowledge, more discerning volition, and more committed action. Clearly, hope is not a feeble wish; it can be a fierce intention. By systematic practice of these three, the soul grows in **HOPE** that its **anticipation** and **expectation** will yield results.

KNOWLEDGE: Named as the first of three essentials for soul progress, it comprises many aspects:

- Knowledge of **why** to do something;
- Knowledge of **how** to do something;
- Material education as with all animals, to earn its livelihood;
- Human education to raise the institutions of civilized society;
- Divine education on the gifts of God which include human virtues and eternal life;
- Wisdom guiding the right use of knowledge; and

- The Truth which conforms to ultimate Reality as taught by the Manifestations of God.

WILL: Human volition is free to turn aside from divine counsels or to choose the path to fulfilment.

- A human soul can escape the animal's fixed, niche-specific behaviours;
- A soul can make significant choices in this world which are not available in the next;
- A soul's volition can be paralyzed by apathy, lethargy, indifference, or fear of annihilation;
- A soul can learn to strive and to endure, to perseverance, and find the will to advance;
- Aligning to Divine Will not only protects from error, but also galvanizes human will power;
- The Manifestations of God modelled by Their lives how to surrender all to the Will of God;
- 'Abdu'l-Bahá molded His will into absolute servitude to Bahá'u'lláh and His Revelation.

ACTION: Human actions do more than change the material world. They transform self and others.

- Actions develop inner and outer Soul coherence;
- Actions that benefit others also benefit the actor;
- Consistent actions invoke the blessings of perseverance;
- Actions provide the dynamic force of example;
- Actions are what gradually transform the world.

The problem remains that while these three factors are *essential*, they are *not sufficient* for the soul to achieve its goal, mainly because *it knows not the definition* of where it is going. How can the creature, limited to creation, define a goal that is beyond attributes? How can the table summon the will to meet the carpenter who created it? How can action, undo the action, that keeps the soul in creation? The conundrum is so profound as to subdue the soul in absolute futility – Subdued, it cries out, "I bear witness to my powerlessness and to Thy might" …whereupon a door opens.

CHAPTER 9

HOW Does Divine Grace Make It All Possible?

We have been following a rational path of questioning the divine, by searching Bahá'í Sacred Writings, to find answers to the WHO, WHAT, WHY, WHEN, WHERE, and HOW of souls who are transforming through a process of awakening to spiritual reality and growing within it. We saw that aspiring human seekers can continuously achieve degrees of spiritual transformation as they move gradually from identifying as mortal to identifying as immortal beings.

We discovered that the HOW of this process begins with interaction of three dynamics: acquisition of relevant knowledge, freely chosen intentions, and suitable action. The final, and most essential element for transforming souls is divine confirmation. Understanding this final element requires a thought process similar to the one needed to solve a Rubik's cube: turning and adjusting, turning and adjusting our understanding – because divine grace is concurrently the means, the end, the initiation, the conclusion and the all-there-is, of spiritual transformation.

Providence * Grace * Confirmation *
Assistance * Divine Bestowals

Providence and Grace

Not surprisingly, the Latin origins of "providence" are "pro" meaning before or in advance of, and "videre" meaning to see. So it actually means "to see ahead." Hence, it is often said that the divine knows our need before we ask. It sees ahead and "provides" the supplies, or prepares the way. The divine perfection of matching creature with environment plays with our sense of time, asking us: did streams appear first and fish just arrive later, or did the intention of fish require that the way be prepared with streams? Sacred Writings describe a divine, loving kindness and care-taking that anticipated the needs of each thing before its arrival and provided those requirements—making those beings possible. Whether you accept divine intention or not, the streams were, in fact, here before the fish arrived.

Sacred Writings caution us to look on all things with that same loving, protective kindness.

> "Look not upon the creatures of God except with the eye of kindliness and of mercy, for Our loving providence hath pervaded all created things, and Our grace encompassed the earth and the heavens."[174]

Sacred Writings sometimes employ analogies that were first revealed to peoples in hot climates, where excessive sun can be dangerous, and shade can mean life-saving protection. In such divine sanctuary, souls may be enabled to enjoy divine beauty by day and by night.

> "We beseech God to extend wide His shadow, that the true believers may hasten thereunto and that His sincere lovers may seek shelter therein. May He bestow upon men blossoms from the bowers of His grace and stars from the horizon of His providence."[175]

HOW DOES DIVINE GRACE MAKE IT ALL POSSIBLE?

Providence is one of the many terms alluding to the concept of divine grace – so much so that it is used in many prayers and contemplations as a title for God itself, as in

> "O Divine Providence! All existence is begotten by Thy bounty..."[176]

Providence is also depicted as the location of God, as in:

> "the heaven of divine providence,"[177] or "the horizon of divine providence."[178]

When "providence" is used in relation to spiritual confirmation it takes the form of a divine emanation or flow, as in

> "the soft-flowing stream of divine providence."[179]

or again as when asking that...

> "the breezes of providence may waft over him."[180]

The effect of the flow of divine providence is to awaken the sleeping consciousness of a soul in the
same way that life is awakened from sleeping seeds by the downpouring of rain.

> "The Kingdom of God is like unto a farmer who comes into possession of a piece of pure and virgin soil. Heavenly seeds are scattered therein, the clouds of divine providence pour down and the rays of the Sun of Reality shine forth."[181]

When the divine provides grace to a person or project, that grace both confirms the intention and supplies the assistance necessary to make that intention a possibility.

"O Lord! I am a broken-winged bird and desire to soar in Thy limitless space. How is it possible for me to do this save through Thy providence and grace, Thy confirmation and assistance."[182]

Now this idea of "confirming" as somehow reinforcing or galvanizing intention, and increasing its probability of success, calls for some considerable elaboration.

Confirmation as a Continuous Process

Universally, traditions are found in which rituals and ceremonies *confirm* that youth have come of age to take moral responsibility for themselves. The confirmation ceremonies are a kind of social proof, witnessed by their respective communities, that the individuals now voluntarily testify to the ethics of their spiritual path or community affiliation. Of course, the degree of spiritual depth and validity that each ceremony holds is known only to God. But as far as the world is concerned, those youth now have some credentials as adult members of their spiritual and social communities.

The meaning of "confirmation" you will find in this chapter, as found in excerpts from Baha'i Sacred Texts, is something quite different from the rituals described above. One remarkable difference is that the confirmations mentioned in Bahá'í teachings happen not once, but continuously, lifelong, day by day, and even moment by moment. And unlike social confirmations, these spiritual ones do not witness or affirm a symbolic ritual of passage. It would be more accurate to say that the divine confirmation found in these Writings actually brings unfoldment of the soul into being. Unfoldment of the soul's attribute no matter how much knowledge, will or action has gone into it – does not yet exist—until it is confirmed by divine acceptance. In this way, the confirmation is concurrently the means and the end of spiritual transformation. (The Rubik's Cube begins to emerge.)

At times, the beneficial effect on our human condition is referred to as a gift or "bounty" which strengthens both the intentions and actions of those who, believing in divine guidance, are trying to live accordingly. Such divine grace be called upon not only for oneself, but also for the benefit of others as 'Abdu'l-Bahá does here:

> "Continually this wanderer [referring to Himself] supplicates and entreats at the threshold of His Holiness the One and begs assistance, bounty and heavenly confirmations in behalf of the believers. You are always in my thoughts. You are not, nor shall you ever be, forgotten."[183]

When such entreaty brings a favorable response, the resulting benefit is referred to as a divine bestowal. It becomes apparent that the idiom, divine grace, is being used to allude to both the agent and the action of what many readers will recognize as the Holy Spirit—without which humanity is unable to manifest its spiritual essence.

> "...the world of humanity is in need of the confirmations of the Holy Spirit. True distinction among mankind is through divine bestowals and receiving the intuitions of the Holy Spirit. If man does not become the recipient of the heavenly bestowals and spiritual bounties, he remains in the plane and kingdom of the animal... Therefore, if a man is bereft of the intuitive breathings of the Holy Spirit, deprived of divine bestowals, out of touch with the heavenly world and negligent of the eternal truths, though in image and likeness he is human, in reality he is an animal..."[184]

Earnest Search Attracts Confirmations

It seems to be a human tendency to expect that *achievement* is what earns reward. But in divine calculations it seems that earnest *search* –the very quest to find the means of soul development—can itself earn the reward of confirmation, described here as the reward of knowledge and certitude.

> "Only when the lamp of search, of earnest striving, of longing desire, of passionate devotion, of fervid love, of rapture, and ecstasy, is kindled within the seeker's heart, and the breeze of His loving-kindness is wafted upon his soul, will the darkness of error be dispelled, the mists of doubts and misgivings be dissipated, and the lights of knowledge and certitude envelop his being."[185]

Here we see that the way earnest search is confirmed, or rewarded, is with the satisfaction of a knowledge that is so sure, it is called "certitude", not just in the mind, but a certitude in the seeker's whole being. That certitude overflows like an overly-filled vessel with an entirely new sense of being, an awareness of new faculties, a sudden penetration of understanding, and an awareness of the entire universe bursting into blossoms of divine presence.

> "Then will the manifold favors and outpouring grace of the holy and everlasting Spirit confer such new life upon the seeker that he will find himself endowed with a new eye, a new ear, a new heart, and a new mind. He will contemplate the manifest signs of the universe, and will penetrate the hidden mysteries of the soul. Gazing with the eye of God, he will perceive within every atom a door that leadeth him to the stations of absolute certitude. He will discover in all things the mysteries of Divine Revelation and the evidences of an everlasting Manifestation."[186]

So here is the explanation we have been seeking since the first question of the interview about WHO is the soul? At that time, the answer came as a paradox – that the soul is above "egress and regress", that it "is still and yet it soareth" and of whom we heard "there is no transformation." Confirmation thus presents a contrast between the soul's *essence* and its *experiences through association* with a human body. In essence, the soul is ever pure and transcendent, created to live forever in the presence of its Creator. And yet, while associated with a human body, it can experience and demonstrate vast changes to its perceptions, thoughts, speech and behaviour. It can experience despair; and it can soar in hope and fulfilment of hopes. It can transform from one state to another.

The soul now feeling its own unfoldment, emerges from the mysteries of itself, into a new understanding and recognition of itself. So desirable is this condition, that it drives us to the next question: HOW can the seeker attract and increase the number of these incremental transformations?

All Actions, that Are Pleasing to God, Attract Confirmation

Sacred Writings make it clear that the "good pleasure" of God is not something whimsical or arbitrary. The will of the divine for humanity is benevolent, and therefore actions that are beneficial for humanity will be pleasing to the divine, be accepted and attract confirmations and assistance. In this sense, confirmations become the *means* for souls to successfully accomplish their service to others.

> "Occupy thy self, during these fleeting days of thy life, with such deeds as will diffuse the fragrance of divine good-pleasure, and will be adorned with the ornament of His acceptance."[187]

> "To engage in some profession is highly commendable, for when occupied with work one is less likely to dwell on

the unpleasant aspects of life. God willing thou mayest experience joy and radiance, gladness and exultation in any city or land where thou mayest happen to sojourn… I fain would hope He may vouchsafe divine assistance and grant confirmation in that which is pleasing and acceptable unto Him."[188]

At times, souls who are seeking guidance may be at a loss to know which service to undertake, or where to place commitment. At these times, souls ask, or even beg, for divine guidance to perceive the right path to take in life. This means that the grace of divine guidance is needed even to *begin* undertakings (let alone accomplish them); and in this sense, divine grace *initiates* the process of transformation that will occur through service to others.

"O Thou kind Lord! …Thou hast shown the way to those who have gone astray; Thou hast led those with parched lips to the fountain of guidance…"[189]

Clearly then, all services that relieve human suffering or advance human well-being will attract confirmation. Could it be that one particular action is of the greatest service to fellow humans? It would have to be something that relieves the greatest suffering a soul can experience. That would be difficult to detect amid the numberless forms of inhumanity and oppression that occur in this life. But there might be one oppression so dismal that it is in a category of its own.

"What 'oppression' is more grievous than this, that a soul seeking the truth, and wishing to attain unto the knowledge of God, should know not where to go for it and from whom to seek it?"[190]

What could relieve that bottomless, grievous oppression?

Most Pleasing of All Is to Share a New and Wider Hope for Humanity

It follows that of all the actions we could take to benefit humanity, sharing a new Revelation of faith and hope would be likely to attract the greatest confirmations – because it is the greatest service a soul could render the world. Since all things require knowledge as well as action words alone will be essential but not sufficient; neither willingness to be of service, nor the actual rendering of services to humanity will be sufficient – only through the addition of constant *mindfulness*, or remembrance. of the Source of grace, will confirmations also be continuous.

> "Breathe not a single breath save in remembrance of His love and in recognition of His grace, in the promulgation of His Utterances and the vindication of His Testimonies. Verily, this is the Magnet of divine confirmations. This is the mighty Force which will surely attract heavenly assistance."[191]

In ages past, renunciants, of every historical religious tradition, were known to wander their regions, perhaps with a begging bowl, asking for sustenance from householders, so that they could teach about their spiritual insights. In this new age however, every individual is expected to seek independently for their own answers rather than passively accept the opinions of a spiritual "class." Additionally, the nobility of every human individual is promoted when they are enabled to earn their living in a dignified way, rather than by begging.

In this millennium, a whole new range of methods for earning a living either *require* one to travel the world, or *enable* one to travel the world. Relocating around the world not only promotes the learning and transformation that a soul may be seeking, but also enables them to share the best of their acquired spiritual insights and divine teachings with others, as they move from place to place. In this way, they can cause their travels to become *eternally* meaningful. For what else could a seeker ever do that would reach as far, or last as long, as sharing spiritual truths with fellow seekers? So these Sacred Writings encourage souls to engage wider horizons whenever they can – give up the known for the unknown – in current language "get out of their comfort zone," and with that courageous intention, attract divine assistance and confirmations.

> "Forsaking home and comfort, become a wanderer, roaming the wilderness of the love of God and engaged in the diffusion of His sweet savours. If thou seekest divine assistance, this is the way; if thou yearnest for **confirmations**, this is the path. By the Ancient Beauty! All else save this will eventually result in manifest loss. This, verily, is the truth, and all else naught but error."[192]

Confirmations by the Holy Spirit are what effectively enable each soul to share spiritual insights and teachings that bring understanding, health, and hope to many others.

> "It is my hope that the breaths of the Holy Spirit will so be breathed into your hearts that your tongues will disclose the mysteries, and set forth and expound the inner meanings of the Holy Books; that the friends will become physicians, and will, through the potent medicine of the heavenly Teachings, heal the long-standing diseases that afflict the body of this world…Rest ye assured that the confirmations of the Holy Spirit will descend upon you…"[193]

'Abdu'l-Bahá wrote the following to a woman scholar of the Torah who wanted to teach effectively:

> "I ask of God that with His assistance and strong support thou mayest teach the inner meanings of the Torah with eloquence, understanding, vigor and skill. Turn thy face toward the Kingdom of God, ask for the bestowals of the Holy Spirit, speak, and the confirmations of the Spirit will come."[194]

As it was when 'Abdu'l-Bahá spoke those words in the 20th century, so it is when we read them again in the 21st century, and so it will continue without end—for spiritual truths do not fade or grow weak; they remain forever brilliant and constant.

> "The splendours of divine assistance are shed abroad from the Kingdom of God, and the hosts of heavenly confirmation are continually descending from the throne of the Most High."[195]

As much as a soul may seek divine assistance to teach and share spiritual truths so another may learn, to the same extent does each soul need divine assistance themselves to recognize a *new* spiritual truth when faced with it. All merely human methods of exploring for new knowledge have their limitations and propensity for error. Confirmations of the Holy Spirit, alone, are the means by which a seeking soul is able to recognize conclusively, and firmly accept, something new to them, from divine revelation.

> "Know, therefore, that what the people possess and believe to be true is liable to error. For if in proving or disproving a thing a proof drawn from the evidence of the senses is advanced, this criterion is clearly imperfect; if a rational proof is adduced, the same holds true; and likewise if a traditional proof is given. Thus it is clear that man does not possess any criterion of knowledge that can be relied upon. But the grace of the Holy Spirit

is the true criterion regarding which there is no doubt or uncertainty. That grace consists in the confirmations of the Holy Spirit which are vouchsafed to man and through which certitude is attained."[196]

What we have received so far in answer to the question of HOW divine grace confirms soul transformation is this: In the form of providence, it pervades all things and shelters all things; it awakens sleeping human consciousness and enables it to soar; it continuously bestows assistance and confirmations that enable humans to rise above mere animal consciousness; it confirms the truly seeking soul who demonstrates *"earnest striving, longing desire, and passionate devotion"* with the reward of knowledge and certitude such that the seeker finds they have been endowed with *"a new eye, a new ear, a new heart, and a new mind."*

Having enjoyed the sublime confirmations of *some* knowledge and *some* certitude, the seeking and transforming soul finds that they want more and more of this expanding awareness and understanding. As with all spiritual paths, the awakening soul is called by Bahá'í Sacred Writings from mere contemplation into action in service to their fellow human beings. All actions which are beneficial to others will attract more insight, understanding, and enlightenment; but the greatest confirmation comes to the greatest service – and that is the service that opens the way for others to enter the path of enlightenment. When the awakening soul shares what little it knows with others, it is then granted a greater measure of confirmation. It seems there is no limit to the continuous flow of divine grace, and no obstacle that can resist its force.

Divine Confirmation Is All Powerful; Can Accomplish All Things

In his exposition of the Seven Valleys of spiritual search and the transformations which a soul undergoes, Bahá'u'lláh reveals the

HOW DOES DIVINE GRACE MAKE IT ALL POSSIBLE?

absolute power of divine grace to accomplish all things even in a flash.

> "These journeys have no visible ending in this temporal world, but the detached wayfarer—should invisible confirmation descend upon him…may traverse these seven stages in seven steps, nay rather in seven breaths, nay even in a single breath, should God will and desire it."[197]

From profound ignorance and isolation to enlightenment in the central courts of reality, is surely a very long process of soul transformation that could take more than a whole lifetime. But apparently this is not necessarily so.

> "…for any movement animated by love moveth from the periphery to the center, from space to the Daystar of the universe. Perchance thou deemest this to be difficult, but I tell thee that such cannot be the case, for when the motivating and guiding power is the divine force of magnetism it is possible, by its aid, to traverse time and space easily and swiftly."[198]

Similarly, an instantaneous transformation is reported in Christian history on the day of Pentecost when the power of the Holy Spirit was suddenly seen to emanate around the Apostles of Jesus. At the time, it appeared to be a fiery essence radiating from their place of meeting.

> "After the death of Christ, the Apostles…at Pentecost… gathered together… Then was divine assistance vouchsafed and the power of the Holy Spirit manifested. The spirituality of Christ triumphed and the love of God took hold. On that day they received divine confirmations, and each departed in a different direction to teach the Cause

of God and unloosed his tongue to set forth the proofs and testimonies."[199]

But let us be clear about the source of that spiritual force. Not only did it not emanate *from* them, it also did not *even enter and pass through* them. By relinquishing the ego that resists spirit, they were able to become flaming *mirrors* of spirit.

> "The descent of the Holy Spirit is not like the entrance of air into the human body. It is a metaphor and an analogy rather than a literal image or account. That which is intended is like the descent of the sun into a mirror, that is, when its splendour is reflected therein."[200]

While less dramatic, the lives of every soul can become mirrors of the power of the Holy Spirit. This is the real source of capacity, not any intelligence, will, or action of a human soul save the capacity to reflect all-accomplishing divine grace.

> "Regarding one's lack of capacity and one's undeserving on the Day of Resurrection, this does not cause one to be shut out from gifts and bounties; for this is not the Day of Justice but the Day of Grace, while justice is allotting to each whatever is his due. Then look thou not at the degree of thy capacity, look thou at the boundless favor of Bahá'u'lláh; all-encompassing is His bounty, and consummate His grace."[201]

Remember that we are interrogating Bahá'í Sacred Writings, and will surely find different concepts, meanings and messages from those we have found before – in order to refresh our understanding of spiritual phenomena and gain further insight. A prime example is the phrase "Day of Resurrection" which Bahá'í sources identify as the age in which a Manifestation of the unknowable

Spirit, appears in human history to awaken and raise up those who have eyes to see and ears to hear. Bahá'í teachings recognize that not all human souls will respond with equal alacrity; most souls, in fact, will turn away and resist. Any *justice* or *judgement* as such, is self-imposed by those who respond to the new revelation and those who do not. For those who do *not* respond, there is eternity, so they will eventually find their way. For those who *do* respond, this day of arising becomes a Day of Grace. Those souls are probably surprised to discover that they do not receive the justice they think they deserve, but rather are in the presence of a Grace that bestows on them boundless favor.

So divine Grace can accomplish all things, and in a flash if it is the will of God. But how does an individual soul increase its receptivity to divine Grace? Jesus was clear about this when He taught that one cannot receive more powerful Grace in a weak old mindset which is likened to a dried out old wine skin; one would have to exchange that old mindset for a vibrant, flexible new mindset capable of holding a more robust, inspiring Revelation.

"To Sacrifice" Means Only Letting Go of the Old – To Make Way for the New

It is not surprising to see that a fear of sacrifice arises in those who don't understand how it works. The *noun* sacrifice focuses on the thing lost – like a sacrificial bird, goat, or lamb that was made the sacrifice. But the action verb "to sacrifice" means to exchange something lesser for something more valuable. Consider this example: "she was glad every time she had a chance to sacrifice an hour of useless media scrolling to spend that time walking and talking with him." It's clear that to make room in life for something better means gladly discarding what is less satisfying.

Let's look again at what happened in Christian history when the Holy Spirit descended to reflect from early believers—displacing all their former preoccupations:

> After the death of Christ, the Apostles...detached themselves from the world, forsook their own desires, renounced all earthly comfort and happiness, sacrificed body and soul to their Beloved, left their homes, took leave of all their cares and belongings, and even forgot their own existence... Then was divine assistance vouchsafed and the power of the Holy Spirit manifested.[202]

How dramatically the Apostles are described as off-loading anything that would deny their openness to the divine assistance flowing upon them. They detached, forsook, renounced, took leave, forgot, and eagerly sacrificed every impediment in their way. The very same call to arise is being raised in this day when the Cause of unifying humankind in peace and mutual assistance is so urgent..

> The teachers of the Cause must be heavenly, lordly and radiant. They must be embodied spirit, personified intellect, and arise in service with the utmost firmness, steadfastness and self-sacrifice. In their journeys they must not be attached to food and clothing. They must concentrate their thoughts on the outpourings of the Kingdom of God and beg for the confirmations of the Holy Spirit. With a divine power, with an attraction of consciousness, with heavenly glad tidings and celestial holiness they must perfume the nostrils with the fragrances of the Paradise of Abhá.[203]

It comes back to the all-accomplishing power of divine grace as taught by Bahá'u'lláh in this day. Sacrifice of childish things belonging to a lower human nature is what makes room for the arrival of spiritual energies to assist the higher nature of a soul to arise and serve fellow human beings. Every human feels weak and inadequate until galvanized by the measureless capacity of divine grace. This is why Abdu'l-Baha called on all souls to learn from Bahá'u'lláh and rely on His teachings about the reality of divine bestowals.

> "Wherefore, look not on the degree of your capacity, ask not if you are worthy of the task: rest ye your hopes on the help and loving-kindness, the favors and bestowals of Bahá'u'lláh—may my soul be offered up for His friends! Urge on the steed of high endeavor over the field of sacrifice, and carry away from this wide arena the prize of divine grace."[204]

In Fact, Divine Grace Is All There Is

It is clear that while we may be, in some sense, the author of our own lives, we do so with capacities which we did not create and do not own. Of ourselves, we can neither perform nor own anything.

> "Man's condition is one of utter helplessness and absolute poverty. All might and power belong to God alone..."[205]

> "This station is that of dying to the self and living in God, of being poor in self and rich in the Desired One. Poverty, as here referred to, signifieth being poor in that which pertaineth to the world of creation and rich in what belongeth to the realms of God."[206]

> "Our reliance on the unfailing grace of an all-loving, all-preserving, ever-sustaining, ever-watchful Providence, must, however much we may be buffeted by circumstances, remain unshaken until the very end."[207]

Our greatest hope therefore is to embrace and rely with heart and soul on this condition of complete dependence on Divine Grace.

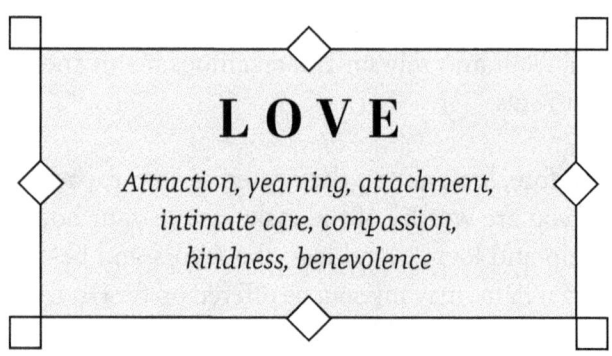

What We Call Divine Grace Is Actually Divine Love in Motion

Whatever your religious affiliation, the flow of divine love is universally the same. Even if you have no religious affiliation, are unsure, or actively decline to believe in God – no worries; God believes in you or you wouldn't exist. And the Great Spirit has proved Its love for you from age to age. This is the ancient message of God, eternal in the past, eternal in the future. As long as there has been humanity, it has been sustained by boundless divine Love; and everyone needs it – for everything, as expressed by 'Abdu'l-Bahá in the following talk, which is formatted to provide you with space for contemplation.

> "There is nothing greater or more blessed than the Love of God!
>
> It gives healing to the sick, balm to the wounded, joy and consolation to the whole world, and through it alone can man attain Life Everlasting.
>
> The *essence* of all religions is the Love of God, and it is the foundation of all the sacred teachings.

It was the Love of God that led Abraham, Isaac, and Jacob, that strengthened Joseph in Egypt and gave to Moses courage and patience.

Through the Love of God, Christ was sent into the world with His inspiring example of a perfect life of self-sacrifice and devotion, bringing to men the message of Eternal Life.

It was the Love of God that gave Muḥammad power to bring the Arabs from a state of animal degradation to a loftier state of existence.

God's Love it was that sustained the Báb and brought Him to His supreme sacrifice, and made His bosom the willing target for a thousand bullets.

Finally, it was the Love of God that gave to the East Bahá'u'lláh, and is now sending the light of His teaching far into the West, and from Pole to Pole.

Thus, I exhort each of you, realizing its power and beauty, to sacrifice all your thoughts, words and actions to bring the knowledge of the Love of God into every heart."[208]

EPILOGUE

The journalist departs from the interview
after months of engagement,
in a condition both dazzled and dazed,
softly muttering words that sound like…
praised be God, the Lord of all worlds…

GLOSSARY

Abhá Beauty
Abhá (Most Glorious) Beauty – a reference to Bahá'u'lláh

Abhá Kingdom
Most Glorious Kingdom – The spiritual counterpart to the material realm, to which it runs parallel and complements. It is as infinite and vast as the whole of material creation. The 'location' for the afterlife (WBF)

Administrative Order
The organisational system of the Bahá'í Faith, which function without clergy or an ecclesiastical structure. It was outlined by Bahá'u'lláh and Abdu'l-Baha, elaborated on by Shoghi Effendi, and is modified and developed from time to time by the Universal House of Justice. (WBF)

Ancient Beauty
Another honorific reference to Bahá'u'lláh

Báb, The
Title meaning The Gate, referring to the Prophet-Herald of the Bahá'í Faith (Siyyid 'Ali-Muhammad, 1819-1850), Forerunner of Bahá'u'lláh, considered by Bahá'ís to be a Manifestation of God in His own right. (CC)

Badasht, Conference of
Gathering of 81 followers of the Báb, for 22 days, near the hamlet of Badasht, June-July 1845, hosted by Bahá'u'lláh. Each day He revealed a new Tablet abrogated former religious laws and repudiated long-established traditions. (DB)

Bahá
Noun, Arabic, meaning Glory.

Bahá'í
Adjective, Arabic, meaning Glorious. Used to describe entities associated with the Bahá'í Faith as in a Bahá'í book, Bahá'í architecture, Bahá'í music, etc.

Bahá'í
In common usage, this adjectival form serves as a noun to identify a Bahá'í person who is a follower of Bahá'u'lláh and member of the Bahá'í community.

Bahá'í Faith
Literally, Glorious Faith, resulting from the Revelation of Bahá'u'lláh.

Bahá'u'lláh
Title meaning The Glory of God, referring to the Prophet-Founder of the Bahá'í Faith (Mírzá Ḥusayn-'Alí, 1817-1892)

Bayán
The epitome of the teachings of the Báb composed in Arabic, during the last few months of His life. (TB)

Blessed Beauty
Another honorific reference to Bahá'u'lláh.

Bird of the Realm of Utterance:
Poetic reference to the Voice of God—as found in the Tablets of Bahá'u'lláh, No. 11. Lawḥ-i-Maqṣúd (Tablet of Maqṣúd)

Covenant
Bahá'u'lláh describes the *Greater Covenant* as the promise that God will periodically provide guidance to humanity as it develops; and *the Lesser Covenant* as the infallible, organizational system which He created to lead His Faith forward in the future. [The reciprocal promise] on the part of humanity is that human beings will accept the divine guidance for their benefit. (WBF)

Central Figures of the Bahá'í Faith is a phrase that refers to the Báb, Bahá'u'lláh, and 'Abdu'l-Bahá.

Centre of the Covenant
Refers to 'Abdu'l-Bah as the appointed successor of Bahá'u'lláh and interpreter of His teachings. (KA, p.145)

Day of Resurrection
According to the Persian Bayan 2:8, revealed by the Báb, this signifies not the end of history but the age when a Manifestation of God provides a new revelation to begin a new stage of development in human history. (WBF)

Guardianship
Divine institution to guard and guide the Cause of God in development of the World Centre of the Faith, spread the teachings of the Cause around the world, and raise up the divinely designated institutions to carry the Faith into the future.

Handmaid
Used often in parallel with "servant" to refer to followers of Bahá'u'lláh, such as: "He, of a truth, desireth that His **servants** and His handmaids should be at peace with one another…" (KA)

Local Spiritual Assembly
Bahá'í administrative institution, annually elected by Bahá'ís of a municipality, in a prayerful atmosphere completely free of nominations or campaigning to serve the local community.

Manifestations of God
The Founders of independent religions who were empowered by God to serve as Divine Educators for humanity. (WBF)

Pen of Glory
Reference to Bahá'u'lláh as channel of divine Revelation

National Spiritual Assembly
Bahá'í administrative institution, annually elected by Bahá'í delegates to a national convention, in a prayerful atmosphere completely free of nominations or campaigning to serve the national community.

Prophet-Herald
Designation that refers to the Báb

Prophet-Founder
Designation that refers to Bahá'u'lláh

Sacred Writings
Although occasional references are made to parallels in the Torah, the Gospels, and the Qur'án, as evidence of universal understandings, for the most part, Sacred Writings as used here, refers to writings of the Báb, Bahá'u'lláh, and 'Abdu'l-Bahá. Some of these Sacred Writings have been translated, interpreted and expounded upon by Shoghi Effendi.

Sadratu'l-Muntahá
Note # 128 in the *Kitab'i'Aqdas*—the Sadratu'l-Muntahá ¶100 Literally "the furthermost Lote-Tree," translated by Shoghi Effendi as *"the Tree beyond which there is no passing."* This is used as a symbol in Islám…to mark the point in the heavens beyond which neither men nor angels can pass in their approach to God, and thus to delimit the bounds of divine knowledge as revealed to mankind. Hence it is often used in the Bahá'í Writings to designate the Manifestation of God Himself.

Shoghi Effendi
First-born grandson of 'Abdu'l-Bahá, designated by him in his Will and Testament to serve as Guardian of the Bahá'í Faith. In that role, Shoghi Effendi translated, interpreted, and expounded upon many of the Bahá'í Sacred Writings.

Tablet
A general term referring to the writings of Bahá'u'lláh, the Báb, and Abdu'l-Bahá. Often they were composed as letters to individuals.

Táhirih
Outstanding follower of the Báb, poetess and teacher of the new revelation, who affirmed the emancipation of women, and suffered martyrdom. Renowned as the only woman among the first eighteen disciples of the Báb.

The Universal House of Justice:
Nine-member, international governing body of the Bahá'í Faith, elected by the members of all National Spiritual Assemblies, every five years, through a process involving no nominations, campaigning, or mention of names. (WBF)

References Consulted for the Glossary

CC *Close Connections*: The Bridge between Spiritual and Physical Reality, by John S. Hatcher, Bahá'í Publishing Trust, Wilmette, 2005.
DB *The Dawn-Breakers*: Nabil's Narrative. Translated by Shoghi Effendi, Bahá'í Publishing Trust, London, UK, 1953, reprinted 1975.
KA *Kitáb-i-Aqdas*: The Most Holy Book. Bahá'u'lláh, Bahá'í World Centre, Haifa, 1992.
TB *The Báb:* The Herald of the Day of Days. H.M Balyuzi, George Ronald, Oxford, UK. 1973, reprinted 1994.
WBF *The World of the Bahá'í Faith*, Ed. by Robert H. Stockman, Routledge, London and New York, 2022.

ENDNOTES

1. Bahá'u'lláh The Hidden Words. Part Two from the Persian. Number 29
2. Bahá'u'lláh Gleanings from the Writings of Baha'u'llah, XCV, p. 194.
3. 'Abdu'l-Bahá Secret of Divine Civilization, p. 1.
4. 'Abdu'l-Bahá, Some Answered Questions, Part 4, No. 58:3, p. 250-251.
5. 'Abdu'l-Bahá, Foundations of World Unity, pp. 73-74.
6. 'Abdu'l-Bahá, Foundations of World Unity, p. 60.
7. Lord Krishna Bhagavad-Gita, VII:2, p.40.
8. 'Abdu'l-Bahá, Selections from the Writings of 'Abdu'l-Bahá, no. 39:2, p. 86.
9. Bahá'u'lláh, Gleanings from the Writings of Bahá'u'lláh , LXXX, p. 155.
10. Bahá'u'lláh, Gleanings from the Writings of Bahá'u'lláh, LXXX, pp. 153-4.
11. Bahá'u'lláh,Gleanings from the Writings of Bahá'u'lláh, LXXX, p. 154.
12. Bahá'u'lláh, Gleanings from the Writings of Bahá'u'lláh, LXXXII, p. 161.
13. Bahá'u'lláh, Gleanings from the Writings of Baha'u'llah, LXXX, p. 154.
14. Bahá'u'lláh, Gleanings from the Writings of Baha'u'llah, LXXXII, p. 161.
15. Bahá'u'lláh, Gleanings from the Writings of Baha'u'llah, LXXXII, p. 161.
16. Apostle Paul, (KJV) First Letter of Paul to the Corinthians, 13:12. Conversely, in the New English Bible, this verse is translated as: "Now we see only puzzling reflections in a mirror, but then we shall see face to face. My knowledge now is partial; then it will be whole, like God's knowledge of me." p. 221.
17. Bahá'u'lláh, Gleanings from the Writings of Baha'u'llah, LXXX, p. 154.
18. Bahá'u'lláh, Gleanings from the Writings of Baha'u'llah, LXXXII, pp. 161-62.
19. Bahá'u'lláh, Gleanings from the Writings of Baha'u'llah, LXXXII, pp. 160-61.
20. The Báb, Selections from the Writings of the Báb, p.98, Persian Bayan, IX, 10.
21. The Báb,Selections from the Writings of the Báb, p.98.
22. Bahá'u'lláh, Days of Remembrance/Naw-Rúz, No. 3, p.12.
23. Bahá'u'lláh, Gleanings from the Writings of Bahá'u'lláh, CXXV, pp. 268-269.
24. 'Abdu'l-Bahá , Secret of Divine Civilization, p. 19.
25. Written on behalf of Shoghi Effendi, Compilation on Living the Life, p. 9.
26. 'Abdu'l-Bahá, Selections from the Writings of 'Abdu'l-Bahá, No. 12.1, p. 30
27. 'Abdu'l-Bahá, Selections from the Writings of 'Abdu'l-Bahá, No. 12.1, p. 30-31

28 'Abdu'l-Bahá, Selections from the Writings of 'Abdu'l-Bahá, No.12.1, p. 31
29 Bahá'u'lláh, Gleanings from the Writings of Bahá'u'lláh, CXVI, p. 248.
30 Bahá'u'lláh, The Hidden Words. Part One from the Arabic, No. 15, p. 7.
31 'Abdu'l-Bahá, Selections from the Writings of 'Abdu'l-Baha, No.197.2, p. 249.
32 Bahá'u'lláh, Bahá'í Prayers/ General Prayers: Steadfastness, p. 185.
33 'Abdu'l-Bahá, Additional prayers revealed by Abdu'l-Baha, "Give me to drink…" https://www.bahai.org/library/authoritative-texts/abdul-baha/additional-prayers-revealed-abdul-baha/482956575/1#196496356
34 Bahá'u'lláh, Prayers and Meditations, No. 87, p. 113.
35 Bahá'u'lláh, Prayers and Meditations, No. 176, p. 204.
36 Bahá'u'lláh, The Call of the Divine Beloved. The Seven Valleys: Contentment, 64, p.40.
37 'Abdu'l-Bahá, The Promulgation of Universal Peace, 04 May 1912, Evanston, Ill., p. 89.
38 Bahá'u'lláh, The Summons of the Lord of Hosts, Suriy-i-Muluk, pp. 207-208.
39 Bahá'u'lláh, Tablets of Baha'u'llah, No. 6 Kalimát-i-Firdawsíyyih (Words of Paradise)
40 Bahá'u'lláh, The Summons of the Lord of Hosts, Suriy-i-Muluk, p. 220.
41 'Abdu'l-Bahá, Paris Talks, 10 Nov. 1911, The Evolution of the Spirit, p. 89.
42 Bahá'u'lláh, Gleanings from the Writings of Bahá'u'lláh: CXXV, p. 267.
43 'Abdu'l-Bahá, Selections from the Writings of 'Abdu'l-Bahá, No. 12.1, p. 31.
44 'Abdu'l-Bahá, Selections from the Writings of 'Abdu'l-Bahá, No. 166, p. 206.
45 Bahá'u'lláh, Hidden Words, Part 2 from the Persian, No. 27, p. 31.
46 'Abdu'l-Bahá, The Promulgation of Universal Peace, 26 May 1912, p. 148.
47 'Abdu'l-Bahá, The Promulgation of Universal Peace, 30 April 1912, Chicago, p. 70.
48 'Abdu'l-Bahá, The Promulgation of Universal Peace, 17 Aug. 1912, Green Acre, Maine, p. 262.
49 'Abdu'l-Bahá, Selections from the Writings of Abdu'l-Baha , No. 38.1, p. 85.
50 'Abdu'l-Bahá, Some Answered Questions, Part 4, No. 64:2, p. 271.
51 'Abdu'l-Bahá, The Promulgation of Universal Peace, 29 Aug. 1912, Malden, Mass., p. 295.
52 'Abdu'l-Bahá, The Promulgation of Universal Peace, Talk in Boston, 24 May 1912, p. 142.
53 'Abdu'l-Bahá, The Secret of Divine Civilization, Bahá'í Publishing Trust, Wilmette, Ill., 1990, pp. 2-3.
54 'Abdu'l-Bahá, Some Answered Questions, Part 4, No. 50:3, p. 226.
55 'Abdu'l-Bahá, Some Answered Questions, Part 4, No. 50:4, pp. 226-227.

ENDNOTES

56 Bahá'u'lláh, Gleanings from the Writings of Bahá'u'lláh, XXVII, p. 65.
57 KJV King James Version of the Bible, Genesis 3:10.
58 The Editors, Merriam-Webster Dictionary. https://www.merriam-webster.com/
59 The Báb, Bahá'í Prayers/Tests and Difficulties, p. 227.
60 Bahá'u'lláh, The Kitáb'i'Aqdas, p.38.
61 Bahá'u'lláh, Tablets of Bahá'u'lláh, No. 15 The Kitáb-i-'Ahd (Book of the Covenant), p. 223.
62 Bahá'u'lláh Tabernacle of Unity, No. 3. Tablet of the Seven Questions, 3:10, p.61.
63 Bahá'u'lláh, Bahá'í Prayers/Spiritual Growth. p.169.
64 Bahá'u'lláh, Gleanings from the Writings of Bahá'u'lláh, XLV, p. 99.
65 Bahá'u'lláh, Gleanings from the Writings of Bahá'u'lláh, CXXII, p. 260.
66 'Abdu'l-Bahá, The Promulgation of Universal Peace, New York, 02 June 1912, p. 166.
67 Bahá'u'lláh, Gleanings from the Writings of Bahá'u'lláh, CVII, p. 214.
68 Bahá'u'lláh, The Hidden Words, from the Arabic, No. 43, p. 13.
69 Bahá'u'lláh, The Hidden Words, from the Persian, No. 21, p. 29.
70 Bahá'u'lláh, The Hidden Words, from the Arabic, No. 8, p. 5.
71 Bahá'u'lláh, The Hidden Words, from the Persian, No. 43, p. 37.
72 Bahá'u'lláh, Prayers & Meditations, No. 22, p. 18.
73 'Abdu'l-Bahá, The Promulgation of Universal Peace, 26 Oct. 1912, p. 378.
74 Apostle Paul, Letter to the Romans, 12:1-2, in The New English Bible with the Apocrypha, p.204.
75 'Abdu'l-Bahá, Quoted by Shoghi Effendi in Advent of Divine Justice, p. 26.
76 Bahá'u'lláh, Summons of the Lord of Hosts, Suriy-i-Haykal: Napoleon III, p.79.
77 Bahá'u'lláh, Tablets of Bahá'u'lláh, 4: Tarazat (Ornaments), p. 37.
78 Bahá'u'lláh, Tablets of Bahá'u'lláh, 8: Ishraqat (Splendours), p.122.
79 Bahá'u'lláh, Gleanings from the Writings of Bahá'u'lláh, CXXXIX, p. 305.
80 Bahá'u'lláh, Epistle to the Son of the Wolf, p. 119.
81 Bahá'u'lláh, Tabernacle of Unity: Two Other Tablets, 4.6, p. 68.
82 Bahá'u'lláh, Gleanings from the Writings of Bahá'u'lláh, LXXXI, p. 156.
83 Bahá'u'lláh, Gleanings from the Writings of Bahá'u'lláh, LXXXI, pp. 156-157.
84 Bahá'u'lláh, Gleanings from the Writings of Bahá'u'lláh, LXXXI, p. 155.
85 Bahá'u'lláh, The Call of the Divine Beloved: Three Other Tablets, 4.10, p. 67.
86 'Abdu'l-Bahá, Some Answered Questions, Part 4, No. 62:7, p. 267.
87 'Abdu'l-Bahá, Some Answered Questions, Part 4, No. 62:3, p. 266.
88 'Abdu'l-Bahá, Some Answered Questions, Part 4, No. 62:7, pp. 267-268.
89 Bahá'u'lláh, Hidden Words from the Arabic, No. 32.

90 Bahá'u'lláh, Kitáb-i-Iqán, p. 14.
91 Bahá'u'lláh, Gleanings from the Writings of Baha'u'lláh: CXXVI, p. 270-271.
92 'Abdu'l-Bahá, Selections from the Writings of 'Abdu'l-Bahá: No. 35.5, p. 76.
93 'Abdu'l-Bahá Selections from the Writings of 'Abdu'l-Bahá, No. 2.16, p. 13.
94 'Abdu'l-Bahá, Will and Testament of 'Abdu'l-Bahá, Part One, p. 13.
95 'Abdu'l-Bahá, Selections from the Writings of 'Abdu'l-Bahá, No. 1101, p. 142.
96 Compilations I, Excellence in All Things: Extract 813, From letters written on behalf of Shoghi Effendi, p. 382.
97 'Abdu'l-Bahá, Paris Talks, Nov. 10, 1911, The First Principle: the Search After Truth, p. 136.
98 'Abdu'l-Bahá, The Promulgation of Universal Peace, Sacramento, 25 Oct. 1912, p. 375.
99 'Abdu'l-Bahá, Selections from the Writings of 'Abdu'l-Bahá. No. 227, p. 309.
100 'Abdu'l-Bahá The Promulgation of Universal Peace, Pittsburgh, 07 May 1912, p. 109.
101 'Abdu'l-Bahá, The Promulgation of Universal Peace, San Francisco, 12 Oct. 1912, p. 366.
102 'Abdu'l-Bahá, Tablets of the Divine Plan, Tablet 14, p. 101.
103 'Abdu'l-Bahá, Tablets of the Divine Plan, Tablet 14, p. 102.
104 Bahá'u'lláh, Epistle to the Son of the Wolf, p. 13.
105 'Abdu'l-Bahá, Paris Talks, Nov. 10, 1911, The Evolution of the Spirit, p. 90
106 'Abdu'l-Bahá The Promulgation of Universal Peace, Boston, Mass., 23 July 1912, pp. 238-239.
107 'Abdu'l-Bahá, The Promulgation of Universal Peace, Washington, D.C., 09 Nov.1912, p. 411.
108 'Abdu'l-Bahá, The Promulgation of Universal Peace, New York, 18 June 1912, p. 206.
109 'Abdu'l-Bahá, The Promulgation of Universal Peace, Washington, D.C., 07 Nov. 1912, p. 400.
110 'Abdu'l-Bahá, The Promulgation of Universal Peace, St. Paul, 20 Sept. 1912, p. 329.
111 'Abdu'l-Bahá, The Promulgation of Universal Peace, 30 May 1912, New York, p. 156.
112 'Abdu'l-Bahá, The Promulgation of Universal Peace, 12 May 1912, New York, p. 121.
113 'Abdu'l-Bahá, Some Answered Questions, Part 5, No. 84:10, p. 346.
114 'Abdu'l-Bahá Some Answered Questions, Part 5, No. 84
115 Bahá'u'lláh, Epistle to the Son of the Wolf, pp. 26-27
116 Bahá'u'lláh, The Hidden Words: Part One – From the Arabic. No. 69, p. 20.

ENDNOTES

117 'Abdu'l-Bahá, Some Answered Questions, Part 4, No. 50:3, p. 226.
118 Bahá'u'lláh, Gleanings from the Writings of Bahá'u'lláh: LII, p. 104.
119 Editors, Merriam-Webster Dictionary, https://merriam-webster/dictionary/talisman
120 Bahá'u'lláh, Gleanings from the Writings of Bahá'u'lláh, CXXII, pp. 259-60.
121 'Abdu'l-Bahá, Some Answered Questions, Part 1, No. 3:5-7, p. 9.
122 'Abdu'l-Bahá, Secret of Divine Civilization, p.109
123 'Abdu'l-Bahá, Selections from the Writings of 'Abdu'l-Bahá, no. 126.1, p. 151.
124 'Abdu'l-Bahá, Foundations of World Unity, p.107
125 'Abdu'l-Bahá, Secret of Divine Civilization, p. 3
126 'Abdu'l-Bahá, Selections from the Writings of 'Abdu'l-Bahá, no. 214.2, p. 280.
127 'Abdu'l-Bahá, Selections from the Writings of 'Abdu'l-Bahá: no. 213.1, p. 280.
128 'Abdu'l-Bahá, The Promulgation of Universal Peace: Dublin, NH, 5Aug. 1912: p. 247.
129 'Abdu'l-Bahá, Some Answered Questions, Part 3, No. 45:3, p. 198.
130 Bahá'u'lláh, The Kitab'i'Iqan/ Part Two, pp. 183-184.
131 'Abdu'l-Bahá, The Promulgation of Universal Peace, Montreal, Canada, 1 Sept 1912: p. 297.
132 Joint Committee, The New English Bible with the Apocrypha. The Gospel: John, 3:7, p.113.
133 'Abdu'l-Bahá, Foundations of World Unity, p. 70.
134 'Abdu'l-Bahá, The Promulgation of Universal Peace, 9 June, 1912, Philadelphia, p. 178.
135 Bahá'u'lláh, Gleanings from the Writings of Bahá'u'lláh, LXXVII, p. 149.
136 Bahá'u'lláh, Bahá'í Prayers and Meditations, No. 150, p. 184.
137 'Abdu'l-Bahá, Paris Talks, p. 66.
138 Shoghi Effendi, Citadel of Faith, p. 149.
139 'Abdu'l-Bahá, Paris Talks. Nov. 24, 2011, p. 114.
140 'Abdu'l-Bahá, The Promulgation of Universal Peace, 04 May, 1912, Philadelphia, p. 89.
141 'Abdu'l-Bahá, Selections from the Writings of 'Abdu'l-Bahá, pp. 124-5.
142 Bahá'u'lláh, Gleanings from the Writings of Bahá'u'lláh, CLIX, p. 336.
143 Bahá'u'lláh, Gleanings from the Writings of Bahá'u'lláh, CLIX, p. 336.
144 'Abdu'l-Bahá, The Promulgation of Universal Peace, Dublin, NH, 06 August 1912, p.251.
145 'Abdu'l-Bahá, The Promulgation of Universal Peace, Dublin, NH, 06 August 1912, p. 251.
146 Joint Committee, The New English Bible with the Apocrypha. The Gospel: Matthew, 26:42, p. 37.
147 Bahá'u'lláh, Prayers and Meditations by Baha'u'llah, p. 163.

148 Bahá'u'lláh, Prayers and Meditations by Baha'u'llah, p. 6.
149 Bahá'u'lláh, Epistle to the Son of the Wolf, p. 11.
150 Bahá'u'lláh, Gleanings from the Writings of Bahá'u'lláh, XXII, p.54.
151 Shoghi Effendi, World Order of Bahá'u'lláh, p.133.
152 'Abdu'l-Bahá, Selections from the Writings of 'Abdu'l-Bahá, p. 295.
153 'Abdu'l-Bahá, *Star of the West*, Vol. 11, issue 14, dated 23 November 1920.
154 'Abdu'l-Bahá, Tablets of 'Abdu'l-Bahá Abbas, p.659.
155 Bahá'u'lláh, Cited by Shoghi Effendi in Advent of Divine Justice, p. 24.
156 'Abdu'l-Bahá, Tablets of 'Abdu'l-Bahá, Vol. III, p. 507.
157 Bahá'u'lláh, Cited by Shoghi Effendi in Advent of Divine Justice, p. 24.
158 Bahá'u'lláh, The Hidden Words, Part I: From the Arabic, No. 31, p. 11.
159 Bahá'u'lláh, Compilation on Huqúq'u'lláh, p.15.
160 Bahá'u'lláh, Cited by Shoghi Effendi in Advent of Divine Justice, p. 24
161 Bahá'u'lláh, Cited by Shoghi Effendi in The Advent of Divine Justice, p. 19.
162 'Abdu'l-Bahá, Selections from the Writings of 'Abdu'l-Bahá, #124, p. 144.
163 Shoghi Effendi, Advent of Divine Justice: p. 68.
164 Shoghi Effendi, Citadel of Faith: Heights Never Before Attained, p. 153.
165 'Abdu'l-Bahá, Some Answered Questions, Part 4, No. 57:5, p.213.
166 Shoghi Effendi, Citadel of Faith: A Turning Point in American Bahá'í History, p. 121.
167 'Abdu'l-Bahá, Selections from the Writings of 'Abdu'l-Bahá: no. 94.2, p.130.
168 Shoghi Effendi, This Decisive Hour: #160, The Utmost Vigor, Vigilance and Consecration.
169 Bahá'u'lláh, Cited by Shoghi Effendi in Advent of Divine Justice, p. 31.
170 Bahá'u'lláh, Cited by Shoghi Effendi in Advent of Divine Justice, p. 25
171 Bahá'u'lláh, Cited by Shoghi Effendi in Advent of Divine Justice, p. 24
172 'Abdu'l-Bahá, Paris Talks, Oct. 16 + 17, 1911, p. 16.
173 'Abdu'l-Bahá, A Traveler's Narrative, p. 45.
174 Bahá'u'lláh, Gleanings from the Writings of Bahá'u'lláh, XIV, p. 33.
175 Bahá'u'lláh, The Summons of the Lord of Hosts: Súriy-i-Haykal, para. 274, p. 136.
176 Bahá'u'lláh, Prayers and Meditations by Baha'u'llah, No. 173, p. 202.
177 Bahá'u'lláh, Tabernacle of Unity: Part 2. From a Tablet to Mírzá Abu'l-Faḍl, para 2:12, p. 23.
178 Bahá'u'lláh, The Summons of the Lord of Hosts: to Pope Pius IX, para. 124, p. 64.
179 Bahá'u'lláh, The Call of the Divine Beloved: Tablet 6, para. 9, p. 79.
180 Bahá'u'lláh, Gems of Divine Mysteries: Javáhiru'l-Asrár, para. 33, p. 25.
181 'Abdu'l-Bahá, Tablets of the Divine Plan: #9: To the Northeastern States, para. 7, p. 63.

ENDNOTES

[182] 'Abdu'l-Bahá, Tablets of the Divine Plan: #14: To the U.S. and Canada, para.14, p. 107.
[183] 'Abdu'l-Bahá, Tablets of the Divine Plan: #3: To the Baha'is of the Central States, para. 2, p. 15.
[184] 'Abdu'l-Bahá, The Promulgation of Universal Peace. Montreal, 5 Sept. 1912, pp. 316-317.
[185] Bahá'u'lláh, Gleanings from the Writings of Bahá'u'lláh, CXXV, p. 267.
[186] Bahá'u'lláh, Gleanings from the Writings of Bahá'u'lláh, CXXV, p. 267.
[187] Bahá'u'lláh, Epistle to the Son of the Wolf, p. 76.
[188] Bahá'u'lláh, Tablets of Bahá'u'lláh: No. 11, Lawḥ-i-Maqṣúd, p.175.
[189] 'Abdu'l-Bahá, Bahá'í Prayers: General Prayers, p. 212-213.
[190] Bahá'u'lláh, Kitáb-i-Íqán, Part One, p. 21.
[191] 'Abdu'l-Bahá, Additional Tablets, Extracts and Talks, No. 195, "O ye beloved friends of God..."
[192] 'Abdu'l-Bahá, Light of the World: Selected Tablets: 7: He is God O servant of Baha!
[193] 'Abdu'l-Bahá, Selections from the Writings of 'Abdu'l-Bahá: no. 219.5, p.286.
[194] 'Abdu'l-Bahá, Selections from the Writings of 'Abdu'l-Bahá: no. 153.4, p. 187.
[195] 'Abdu'l-Bahá, Compilation for the 2018 Counsellors' Conference: No. 24, from the Persian.
[196] 'Abdu'l-Bahá, Some Answered Questions, Part 5, No. 83.7, p. 345.
[197] Bahá'u'lláh, The Call of the Divine Beloved. The Seven Valleys, para. 87, p. 50.
[198] 'Abdu'l-Bahá, Selections from the Writings of 'Abdu'l-Bahá, No. 166.1, p. 206.
[199] 'Abdu'l-Bahá, Some Answered Questions, Part 2, No. 24:3, p. 120.
[200] 'Abdu'l-Bahá, Some Answered Questions, Part 2, No. 24:2, p. 120.
[201] 'Abdu'l-Bahá, Selections from the Writings of 'Abdu'l-Bahá: No. 153.3, p. 187.
[202] 'Abdu'l-Bahá, Some Answered Questions, Part 2, No. 24:2, p.120.
[203] 'Abdu'l-Bahá, Tablets of the Divine Plan, No. 12, To the Western States, para. 10, p. 88.
[204] 'Abdu'l-Bahá, Selections from the Writings of 'Abdu'l-Bahá, No. 8.5, p. 27.
[205] 'Abdu'l-Bahá, Some Answered Questions, Part 4, No. 70:5, p. 288.
[206] Bahá'u'lláh, The Call of the Divine Beloved. The Seven Valleys:, para 76, p. 45.
[207] Shoghi Effendi, This Decisive Hour: 158 – A God-Given Mandate, 15 June 1946.
[208] 'Abdu'l-Bahá Paris Talks, pp. 82-83. (Note: formatting has been added by the author.)

BIBLIOGRAPHY

Bibliography of Bahá'í Sources

Bahá'u'lláh

_____ *Days of Remembrance:* Selections from the Writings of Bahá'u'lláh for Bahá'í Holy Days. Bahá'í World Centre, Haifa, 2016.

_____ *Epistle to the Son of the Wolf* Translated by Shoghi Effendi, Bahá'í Publishing Trust, Wilmette, Illinois, 1988.

_____ *Gems of Divine Mysteries:* Javáhiru'l-Asrár. Bahá'í World Centre, 2002.

_____ *Gleanings from the Writings of Bahá'u'lláh* Translated from the original written in Arabic and Persian by Shoghi Effendi, Wilmette: Bahá'í Publishing Trust, 1988 [1935]

_____ *Kitáb'i'Íqán: The Book of Certitude* Revealed by Bahá'u'lláh, Translated by Shoghi Effendi, Bahá'í Publishing Trust, Wilmette, Illinois. Pocket sized edition, Bahá'í Publishing Trust, Wilmette, Illinois, reprinted 1989.

_____ *Prayers and Meditations by Bahá'u'lláh.* Compiled and translated by Shoghi Effendi. Bahá'í Publishing Trust, London, UK, Revised edition, 1978.

_____ *Tablets of Bahá'u'lláh:* Revealed after the Kitáb-i-Aqdas. Compiled by the Research Department of the Universal House of Justice, and translated by Habibi Taherzadeh with the assistance of a Committee at the Bahá'í World Centre. Bahá'í Publishing Trust, Wilmette, Illinois, 1988.

_____ *The Call of the Divine Beloved:* Selected Mystical Works of Bahá'u'lláh. Bahá'í Publishing Trust, Wilmette, Illinois, 2018.

_____ *The Hidden Words of Bahá'u'lláh* Translated by Shoghi Effendi with the assistance of some English friends. Bahá'í Publishing Trust, Wilmette, Illinois, reprinted 1985.

_____ *The Kitáb-i-Aqdas: The Most Holy Book.* Haifa: Bahá'í World Centre, 1992.

_____ *The Summons of the Lord of Hosts:* Tablets of Bahá'u'lláh. Bahá'í World Centre, Haifa, 2002.

_____ *The Tabernacle of Unity:* Bahá'u'lláh's Responses to Mánikchí Ṣáḥib and other Writings, Bahá'í World Centre, 2006.

The Báb

_____ *Selections from the Writings of the Báb.* Compiled by the Research Department of the Universal House of Justice. Translated by Habib Taherzadeh, with the assistance of a Committee at the Bahá'í World Centre, Bahá'í World Centre, Haifa

Bahá'u'lláh, The Báb, and Abdu'l-Baha

_____ *Bahá'í Prayers.* A Selection of Prayers Revealed by Bahá'u'lláh, The Báb, and 'Abdu'l-Bahá. Bahá'í Publishing Trust, Wilmette, Illinois, 2002.

Bahá'u'lláh and 'Abdu'l-Bahá

_____ *Bahá'í Scriptures:* Selections from the Utterances of Bahá'u'lláh and 'Abdu'l-Bahá. Approved by Bahá'í Committee on Publications, Second Edition, Brentanos Publishers, New York, 1923. Horace Holley, editor. (Replaced by Bahá'í World Faith, 1943)

_____ *The Divine Art of Living:* Selections from the Writings of Bahá'u'lláh and 'Abdu'l-Bahá. Compiled by Mabel Hyde Paine; revised by Anne Marie Scheffer. New edition 1986 by the National Spiritual Assembly of the Baha'is of the United States. Bahá'í Publishing Trust, Wilmette, Ill. USA

Abdu'l-Bahá

_____ *A Traveler's Narrative.* Written to illustrate the episode of the Báb. Bahá'í Publishing Trust, Wilmette, Illinois, USA. 1980.

_____ *'Abdu'l-Bahá in London* Bahá'í Publishing Trust, UK. 1982 reprint

_____ *Additional Prayers Revealed by 'Abdu'l-Bahá.* https://www.bahai.org/library/authoritative-texts/abdul-baha/additional-prayers-revealed-abdul-baha/

BIBLIOGRAPHY

_____ *Additional Tablets, Extracts and Talks*. (97 recently translated texts) https://www.bahai.org/library/authoritative-texts/abdul-baha/additional-Tablets-extracts-talks/

_____ *Foundations of World Unity* – Compiled from Addresses and Tablets of 'Abdu'l-Bahá. Bahá'í Publishing Trust, Wilmette, Illinois. Copyright 1945, 1972 by the National Spiritual Assembly of the Baha'is of the United States. Sixth printing, 1979.

_____ *Paris Talks*. Addresses given by 'Abdu'l-Bahá in Paris in 1911. Bahá'í Publishing Trust, U.K. Eleventh British Edition, 1969, reprinted 1979.

_____ *Selections from the Writings of 'Abdu'l-Bahá* Compiled by the Research Department of the Universal House of Justice. Translated by a Committee at the Bahá'í World Centre and by Marzieh Gail. Bahá'í World Centre. Bahá'í Publishing Trust, Wilmette, Illinois, 2014.

_____ *Some Answered Questions*. Collected and translated from the Persian by Laura Clifford Barney. Newly Revised by a Committee at the Bahá'í World Centre. Bahá'í Publishing Trust, Wilmette, Illinois, 2014.

_____ *Tablets of 'Abdu'l-Bahá Abbas*: Vol. I, pp.1-238. Bahá'í Publishing Society, Chicago, USA. First Edition 1915, Second Edition, 1919. Reproduced online at *https://bahai-library.com/writings/abdulbaha/tab/1.html*

_____ *Tablets of 'Abdu'l-Bahá Abbas*: Vol. II, pp.239-484. Bahá'í Publishing Society, Chicago, USA. First Edition 1915, Second Edition, 1919. Reproduced online at *https://bahai-library.com/writings/abdulbaha/tab/2.html*

_____ *Tablets of 'Abdu'l-Bahá Abbas*: Vol. III, pp.485-730. Bahá'í Publishing Society, Chicago, USA. First Edition 1915, Second Edition, 1919. Reproduced online at *https://bahai-library.com/writings/abdulbaha/tab/3.html*

_____ *Tablets of the Divine Plan*. Bahá'í Publishing Trust, Wilmette, Illinois. First pocket edition, 1993.

_____ *The Promulgation of Universal Peace*. Talks delivered by 'Abdu'l-Bahá during His visit to the United States and Canada in 1912. Bahá'í Publishing Trust, Wilmette, Illinois, USA, 1982

_____ *The Secret of Divine Civilization.* Translated from the Persian text by Marzieh Gail in consultation with Ali-Kuli Khan. Bahá'í Publishing Trust, Wilmette, Illinois. Copyright 1990 by the National Spiritual Assembly of the Bahá'ís of the United States of America. First pocket-sized Edition.

_____ *Will and Testament of 'Abdu'l-Bahá.* Bahá'í Publishing Trust, Wilmette, Illinois, 1990.

Shoghi Effendi

_____ *Advent of Divine Justice.* Bahá'í Publishing Trust, Wilmette, Illinois, 1990.

_____ *Arohanui:* Letters from Shoghi Effendi to New Zealand. Bahá'í Publishing Trust of Suva, Fiji Islands, 1982 edition.

_____ *Bahá'í Administration:* Selected Messages 1922-1932, Bahá'í Publishing Trust, Wilmette, Illinois, 1974.

_____ *Citadel of Faith:* Messages to America 1947-1957. Baha'i Publishing Trust, Wilmette, Illinois, USA, 1965.

_____ *Dawn of a New Day* – Letters from Shoghi Effendi to India and Burma Bahá'í Publishing Trust of India, New Delhi, 1970.

_____ *Lights of Guidance:* A Bahá'í Reference File, compiled by Helen Bassett Hornby, Bahá'í Publishing Trust, New Dehi, India. Third Edition, 1994.

_____ *This Decisive Hour:* Messages from Shoghi Effendi to the North American Bahá'ís, 1932 to 1946. Bahá'í Publishing Trust, Wilmette, Illinois, 2002.

_____ *Unfolding Destiny:* Messages from the Guardian of the Bahá'í Faith to the Bahá'í Community of the British Isles. Bahá'í Publishing Trust, 1981 edition.

_____ *The World Order of Bahá'u'lláh* – Selected Letters by Shoghi Effendi. Bahá'í Publishing Trust, Wilmette, Illinois, 60091 Second revised edition, 1974

BIBLIOGRAPHY

The Universal House of Justice

_____ *The Institution of the Counsellors*. Bahá'í Publications Australia, 2001.

_____ *The Prosperity of Humankind*. Bahá'í International Community's Office of Public Information, Haifa. 1995.

_____ *The Promise of World Peace*. Message addressed to the Peoples of the World, October 1985. Reprinted as *A Bahá'í Statement on Peace*, by the Association for Bahá'í Studies, Ottawa, Ontario, Canada. 1986.

_____ *TURNING POINT* Selected Messages of the Universal House of Justice *and Supplementary Material*, 1996-2006. Palabra Publications, 2006.

_____ Letter to the Bahá'ís of the World, Riḍván 2023.

_____ Letter to the Followers of Bahá'u'lláh in the United States of America, 29 Dec. 1988.

_____ Letter to the National Spiritual Assembly of the Bahá'ís of Canada, 25 July 1988.

Bahá'í International Community

_____ *The Prosperity of Humankind*. Bahá'í International Community's Office of Public Information, Haifa. 1995

Bahá'í World Centre

_____ *Bahíyyih Khánum, the Greatest Holy Leaf:* A Compilation from Bahá'í Sacred Texts, Writings of the Guardian of the Faith, and Bahíyyih Khánum's Own Letters, made by the Research Department at the Bahá'í World Centre. 1982.

_____ *Compilation on Huqúq'u'lláh*, prepared by the Research Department of the Universal House of Justice, published by the National Spiritual Assembly of the Bahá'ís of Canada, 2017.

_____ *Compilation on Living the Life*, in "The Compilation of Compilations" Volume II, Bahá'í Publications Australia, 1991.

_____ *Excellence in All Things*, in "The Compilation of Compilations" Volume I, Bahá'í Publications Australia, 1991.

_____ *The Institution of the Mashriqu'l-Adhkar*: A Statement & Compilation by the Research Department of the Universal House of Justice, 2017.

_____ *To Set the World in Order: Building and Preserving Strong Marriages*. A Compilation Prepared by the Research Department of the Universal House of Justice, August 2023

_____ *Trustworthiness: A Cardinal Bahá'í Virtue*. Compiled by the Research Department of the Universal House of Justice, 1987, revised 1990.

National Spiritual Assembly of the Bahá'ís of Australia

_____ *Gemstone: A Programme in Living a Bahá'í Life*, 1986

National Spiritual Assembly of the Baha'is of the United States of America

_____ *Bahá'í Personal Transformation Program*, (1973)

Bibliography of Individual Authors

Arnold, Sir Edwin. Translator from the Sanskrit of *The Song Celestial*, or Bhagavad-Gita (from the Mahabharata), Routledge & Kegan Paul, London, UK. 1964

Editors. *Merriam-Webster Dictionary*. An Encyclopedia Britannica Company, since 1828. https://www.merriam-webster.com

Esslemont, J.E. *Bahá'u'lláh and the New Era:* An Introduction to the Bahá'í Faith. Bahá'í Publishing Trust, Wilmette Illinois. Copyright 1950, 1970, 1976, 1980 by the National Spiritual Assembly of the Bahá'ís of the United States.

Fuller, R. Buckminster. *An Operating Manual for Spaceship Earth.* Touchstone Books, 1969.

Holley, Horace, ed. *Bahá'í Scriptures: Selections from the Utterances of Bahá'u'lláh and 'Abdu'l-Bahá.* Approved by Bahá'í Committee on Publications, 1923. Second edition. Brentano's Publishers, New York.

BIBLIOGRAPHY

Joint Committee on the New Translation of the Bible. *The New English Bible with the Apocrypha.* Oxford University Press, NY, 1971.

Khan, Peter. *The Sacred and The Nature of Transformation* Talk given 23 May 1991, Seat of the Universal House of Justice

McCreary, Elaine. *Our Seven Families: Expanding and Enriching our Sense of Belonging.* Selections from Baha'i Sacred Writings. George Ronald Publishers, Oxford, UK, 2018.

Ward, Barbara. *Spaceship Earth.* Columbia University Press, New York, 1966

ABOUT THE AUTHOR

Peering through phenomena to feel the noumena behind them was a practice Elaine began in late childhood, long before finding words to name what she was doing.

She augmented her FAITH as a Christian child, with 19 years in early adulthood, building HOPE in soul growth through the practice of Raja Yoga which combined methods of body, mind, heart, and right action to draw her soul closer to its Beloved goal.

Then, as a tenured professor, she was introduced by her graduate students to Bahá'í Sacred Writings and found in them a conduit for the wealth of divine LOVE that is at once the source, sustainer, and goal of every human soul.

Being by both nature and training, a learner, professor and facilitator of lifelong learning, she has dedicated herself to sharing insights on the universal human condition, found in these Sacred Writings that are at once so familiar and so surprisingly fresh.

www.ingramcontent.com/pod-product-compliance
Lightning Source LLC
Chambersburg PA
CBHW060527090426
42735CB00011B/2405